MUSIC AND THE CHURCH

DAVID B. PASS

BROADMAN PRESS
Nashville, Tennessee

ISBN: 0-8054-6814-5
Dewey Decimal Classification: 783
Subject Heading: CHURCH MUSIC
Library of Congress Catalog Number: 88-7521
Printed in the United States of America

Unless otherwise stated, all Scripture quotations are from HOLY BIBLE: *New International Version*, copyright © 1978, New York Bible Society. Used by permission.

Library of Congress Cataloging-in-Publication Data

Pass, David B., 1950-
  Music and the church.

  Bibliography: p.
  1. Church music.   2. Music—Philosophy and aesthetics.
I. Title.
ML3001.P18   1989   264'.2   88-7521
ISBN 0-8054-6814-5

Contents

Introduction

There is a lot of evidence today that Christians are struggling to relate in a Christian way to the musical styles of their culture. Witness the furor in recent years created by evangelists advocating the destruction of rock music records by Christian young people. Then there is the controversy surrounding "backward masking," the alleged subliminal references to Satan being programmed into certain records.[1] When we move into the area of church music, even more dissension is evident. Are popular musical styles appropriate in the church? Can the gospel be properly communicated by using rock music (for example, "heavy metal" music)? Are choirs no longer relevant? What is the place of the soloist in the church? Has the recent revolution in worship made all uses of music other than praise music obsolete?[2]

The questions continue, the debate rages on, with Christians rejecting other Christians based on certain musical styles. It is no wonder then that Bill Gaither recently stated that, in his opinion, there was no more divisive issue in the church at present than the issue of music.[3]

There is, in my opinion, no reason for this state of affairs. The Bible very clearly provides us with the principles needed to solve these controversies. However, there are no prepackaged answers or special verses we can turn to. Only by carefully studying the Bible, theology, and many other disciplines can one attempt to form a coherent theology of music and church music. This book is the result of such an attempt. I believe that we must have such a theology. Without it we will never know how music relates to our Christian lives and why it is so important to us as individuals and to us together as the body of Christ.

There are three groups of people to whom I write: the musical leadership of Christian churches in the Western world; those involved in developing indigenous church song and music in the non-Western world; and all of those involved in contemporary Christian music. In my opinion all three groups have a vital contribution to make, and I believe that what they will find in these pages will encourage them and equip them for their respective tasks.

After stating the problems caused by the lack of a theology of music and church music, I will develop a theology of music in general and then a theology of church music. Do not be put off by the word *theology*. A Christian is "doing theology" all the time, often without being aware of it. When you tell someone that Jesus loves them, that is a theological statement. When you ponder over the will of God for you as you face a certain decision, you are doing theology. Admittedly, this is not theology in a formal sense, as one would study in a seminary. Yet it is nonetheless theology—reflection on the implications of the Christian faith for my life and my world. I have used a number of diagrams in this book because I find it helps make some ideas more concrete and easier to visualize. Hopefully, you will also find it a help as you read through this book. I have a vision about what could happen in church music if we understood its role in our lives: I believe that we could be standing on the edge of a totally unprecedented explosion of church music and Christian music all over the world. God's desire is to save lost humanity, and a key element in that plan is music. Join me in an exciting adventure as we discover God's design for music in our world.

A Question of Method

The approach I am taking in this book differs from the usual approach to church music—discussing the references to music in the Bible and ordering the material in a historical way. The historical approach to church music is so deeply rooted in our culture that many times during the writing of this book, when people would hear that my topic was church music, they would say, "So, you're going to write on the history of church music from the earliest times till now, aren't you?"

As important as biblical references to music and the history of music in the Bible and later times are, one will never derive a theology of church music by simply quoting biblical texts on music and recounting the history of church music. The reason is simple: there is a difference between *descriptive* statements (what *is* or *was* the case), and *normative* statements (what *should be* the case). A *description* of music in the Bible cannot yield *normative*[3a] statements about what the church should be doing with music today. Neither will the history of church music provide us with such norms. It is theology which has the task and the risk of carefully scrutinizing the biblical references to music and much other data, including the history of music, and then coming to an interpretive judgment: This is how the church *should* use music now, today, here. We cannot rest with merely restating all the biblical references to music. The writers and compilers of the Bible did not regurgitate material from the past—they strove to bring it into dynamic and explosive contact with the present. The community of faith in the Judeo-Christian tradition has always done this.[3b] For example, at the Council of Nicea, the early church learned "the necessity of going beyond *scriptural language* to formulate what was considered *scriptural truth.*"[3c] This statement by Bernard Lonergan expresses exactly the approach I want to take in this book. It involves using Scripture in the formation of a *theological theory of church music* so that the implications of the biblical revelation for music and church music are made directly relevant to us today.

A.   The Problem Stated

The problem which I want to address in this book was recently formulated by Harold Best in his paper given to the National Association of Schools of Music, entitled "Church Music Curriculum":

> Excellent church music training must be embedded, not primarily in the nature of music and musical types, standards of practices, and scholarly excellence, but in a bed-rock theological perspective. . . . the discipline of church music has not been subject to the deep perspectival scrutinies that it should. Therefore, the church musician is caught between wondering whether he is a paid amateur, or a volunteer professional. He does not know, philosophically and theologically, what he is about.[4]

Phrases like "a bed-rock [sic] theological perspective," "deep perspectival scrutinies" and "he does not know, philosophically and theologically, what he is about" all suggest that the problem of church music today is that those involved in making decisions about music in the church do not have a rationale for what they are doing.

Best is not alone in assessing the basic problem of church music in this way. Others have also seen the need for a rationale or theory of church music. It is significant that these calls for a theory of church music have not come from theologians, but rather from practicing church and Christian musicians. Here are some examples taken from all three segments relevant to us in this book—Western church musicians, contemporary Christian musicians, and those in cross-cultural church music situations.

1. Writing a prolegomena to a theology of church music, Jay Wilkey (a Southern Baptist) chided fellow church musicians for their lack of interest in a theological theory for their discipline: "Church musicians have developed systematic approaches to the practice of church music, but none have given more than a cursory mention to the idea of a theology of music."[5]

2. Paul Wohlgemuth comes from a Penecostal background and seems to speak for many musicians when he writes: "I would feel more comfortable directing a choir than writing about music, but I feel a need exists for more discourse on church music."[6]

3. Speaking twenty-two years after the Second Vatican Council, Roman Catholic scholar Peter Jeffery insists that in the area of Catholic church music "we continue to lack a comprehensive, carefully worked out program for reform."[7]

4. Lionel Dakers, director of the Royal School of Church Music, emphasizes the confused situation in Anglican church music, calling for "a rational and considered approach which will help deter us from pursuing what might otherwise be blind alleys."[8]

5. Contemporary Christian musician Steve Camp stated recently in an interview: "I just think the average Christian musician knows more about his music than he does about Jesus Christ. He has not put the same effort into his theology as he has into his songwriting—and that goes for everybody."[9]

6. In the field of indigenous non-Western church music, it is unfortunately true that the major missionary move from the West often confused Western culture with Christianity. Missionaries would insist, for example, on church music being a translated version of what the missionary was used to in his or her country of origin.[10] This had the effect of

estranging new converts to Christianity from the music of their own culture.[11] This process has gone for so long now that in Africa for instance, African Christians themselves sometimes reject singing Christian hymns to African music.[12] It is quite clear that the missionaries had developed no rationale at all for the new situation they faced in terms of church music. The results of this seriously hindered the growth of culturally relevant churches in Africa and elsewhere.

These opinions and statements give the impression that those involved in church music do not have a clear idea of the underlying principles, the theory of their discipline. This lack of a theoretical framework seems to have led church music into a number of practical problems, echoing the comments of Heinz Schuster about pastoral theology: "Without solid theory, solid practice is not possible."[13] A few of these practical problems will now be discussed.

B. The Results of the Problem Illustrated

1. As far as the musical "product" is concerned, there is a conviction that many Christian songs today have words of an inferior quality. On this issue, Carl Schalk has recently expressed himself, saying that it is especially its theological content that makes much church music today appalling. Specifically, he mentions its superficial moralism, calling it music in which "the hard word of sin and grace, law and gospel, death and resurrection is—if not obliterated—at least seriously muted."[14] Schalk's assessment of the situation in American Lutheran and other Protestant denominations is paralleled by Peter Jeffery's analysis of Catholic church music. He describes it as a chaotic situation, drawing attention to "the scarcity of high-quality musical settings of theologically sound texts that are suitable for congregational use."[15]

It is clear from these statements that there is little or no agreement on what constitutes appropriate church music, either words or music. This appears to be an example of the effects in *practice* of a vacuum in *theory*. Joseph Gelineau has written that while all music can indeed be religious or sacred, "only that music is specifically Christian which articulates the Christian faith."[16] Church music without a proper theory of its own has no theological vantage point from which to decide whether a certain piece of church music does in fact articulate the Christian faith or not.

2. A second illustration of the problems caused by the lack of a theory of church music is in the area of the training given to church musicians about the theological context in which they work. The late Erik Routley, perhaps the most prolific English hymnologist of this century, considered it common knowledge that institutions training church musicians were "liable to turn out musicians who have carefully laid aside any theological insights they may have had."[17] This kind of training produced musicians who lived "entirely within the world of music," musicians who were theologically naive "to an alarming degree."[18] More recently Bruce Leafblad has remarked that, in general, church musicians have "a limited understanding of, and appreciation for, the true nature and work of the church."[19]

Obviously, church musicians are not receiving the kind of theological formation they need for their task.[20] The corollary is equally true in that ministers of religion usually receive very little help on the musical aspects of church life in their training.[21] The result is that neither of the groups most involved in making decisions about music in the life of the church—ministers and musicians—have an ordered set of principles by which to make those decisions. Once again, the lack of a theoretical framework which could include ministers and church musicians in a common universe of discourse leads to many practical problems of communication in church music.

3. One of the most divisive areas in the practice of church music today concerns what Peter Jeffery has described as "the widespread polarization between classically-trained musicians and those working in styles derived from popular and commercial music."[22] A situation like this can lead to the outright rejection of the church and its message by musicians in one or other of the "opposing" camps. Alternative reactions are either a resentful "toleration" of so-called musical "snobs" or a resignation to so-called musical "mediocrity." Occasionally, a musician will resort to a form of "musical schizophrenia"[23] in which his/her music is kept in a separate and watertight compartment, untouched by whatever church music the musician happens to be involved in. Not only are musicians in the church deeply divided over the issue of musical diversity, churches and even whole denominations define themselves by an unquestioned allegiance to specific styles of music. Paul Wohlgemuth calls this diversity regarding musical tastes among worshipers "one of the perplexing problems in church music today."[24]

At the level of groups of churches (denominations), the British sociologist David Martin was able to detect three large cultural patterns in English Christianity based largely on "those who sing carols, those who sing hymns and those who sing choruses."[25] When a musical style becomes the social badge of one group in the church and is then used as the basis for excluding other Christian groups, then church music deserves the contempt it sometimes receives from devout Christians. A good example of this response was C. S. Lewis who, according to Erik Routley, hated the hymns of the church because "he heard them as the church's gang-songs."[26] Evidently in the case of musical diversity in the church, church music has failed to develop a comprehensive framework within which to integrate diverse and often con-flicting musical styles.

4. Perhaps nowhere else have the problems caused by a nonexistent rationale for church music been more glaring than in the impact on church music caused by the liturgical and charismatic movements this century. These two move-ments have had a tremendous effect on the church in numer-ous ways. While the movements must be seen as somewhat disparate from a historical point of view, both originated from a concern for a more vital Christendom, especially and perhaps solely in the area of worship. It was therefore inevi-table that they would both affect church music profoundly. In fact, these movements have had the effect of completely disrupting the status quo in worship which had existed prior to their ascendance, all within the space of a few decades.

Referring to the effect of the liturgical movement in the Roman Catholic Church which culminated in major liturgi-cal reforms at the Second Vatican Council, Joseph Gelineau remarked that "it was high time the church made an effort to adapt." However, the change in the liturgy was "so sud-den and so radical that it could truly be called a crisis."[27] Musicians in particular were caught without the resources to deal with the changes introduced, as Peter Jeffery has point-ed out: "The revolutions in biblical, patristic, and liturgical studies that paved the way for the reforms of Vatican II had hardly any counterpart in the area of music."[28]

The effects of the charismatic movement on church music have been no less dramatic. According to James White, the dominant characteristics of the Penecostal tradition (which fathered what is now called the "charismatic movement") are "the freedom and spontaneity with which any worship-per can testify, sing, pray, speak in tongues or interpret. . . . Informality has finally triumphed in Pentecostal wor-ship."[29] At the heart of its informality is a desire for more authentic worship. In the words of Paul Wohlgemuth, "we might say it [i.e., Pentecostal worship] is worship-worship," not doing-worship.' "[30] Such a radical reconceptualization of worship (compared with previous ideas of worship) simply had to affect the music used in these traditions—and it has. Observations in a number of churches suggest that there is possibly an entire generation of new converts to Christianity within the charismatic orbit who have little or no knowledge of what used to be called the "great hymns of the faith." In many charismatic churches, "Scripture choruses" have largely displaced the traditional hymnody of the church, for better or worse.

Both the liturgical and charismatic movements coincide in that they demand more meaningful worship and insist on more active participation by everyone in the congregation. The corresponding impact on church music has been twofold: First, there has been a proliferation of vast masses of music assumed to be more relevant to contemporary needs than the traditional materials previously available. In the second place, restrictions have been placed on choral and specialized musical performances during times of worship so as to ensure greater congregational participation in the music of the church. Robert Hayburn has provided a recent description of the musical situation in many churches which has resulted from these reform movements. Although his assessment is perhaps a little on the pessimistic side, it does suggest that some things of value may have been lost for the church in the spate of reforms:

> Choirs have disappeared from many a church. Almost everyone is making music in the church, except trained musicians. Now one hears only unison singing, dull in style, and often secular in type and no different from that heard at ball games, football rallies, and picnics.[31]

In short, the evidence suggests that without a coherent

theory of its own, church music is powerless to evaluate its own distinctive role in the face of the aggressive reforms which have swept through the church this century.

5. In concluding this discussion of some of the practical problems which result from the absence of a carefully formulated theory of church music, it is clear that church music cannot afford to be resistant to change or simply change for change's sake. The two options of traditionalism and progressivism, in church music as elsewhere in the church are excluded.[32] The only viable alternative is to develop a comprehensive theory of church music which will enable church music to assess itself, the church, and changed cultural situations with a measure of detachment and objectivity.

Unfortunately, apart from the seminal and as yet largely untranslated works of Oskar Söhngen,[33] there does not exist a proper theory of church music that would meet current needs. Even Sohngen's contributions are perhaps overly historical in their approach to church music, at the expense of systematic dimensions. In a recent discussion of the field, Victor Gebauer came to the conclusion that "there is no satisfactory review of the theology of music or church music in the English language."[34] Not even the voluminous works on church music of Erik Routley can be said to constitute a theory of church music. This fact was correctly observed by Jay Wilkey, who drew attention to the fact that although Routley had written profusely and even brilliantly, he had never developed a systematic approach to church music.[35]

We are therefore left without a theory of church music appropriate to the needs of English-speaking Christianity in the West, although, as previously indicated, there is an urgent need for one.[36] In addition to specific practical problems, there are also sound reasons of a more general nature why such a theory of church music should be developed.

C. Reasons in Support of a Theory for Church Music

First, without a theory of church we have no way to reflect
critically on the practice of church music. We are then at the
mercy of what has been described as "ideological practice."[37] Ideological practice is the practice of someone who
believes that practice can exist without any underlying theory or principles whatsoever, a "pure" practice, unmixed
with, and untainted by, theory.[38] The truth is, however, that
"theory is always (though perhaps unconsciously) in-
fluenced by practice, and practice in its turn is always
(though equally unconsciously) determined by theory."[39]
The failure to realize this relationship between theory and
practice often leads to an uninformed or ideological practice.
Here one is looking for "regurgitated, easily digestible ideas
which can be immediately used in practice without consid-
ering the reflection that led to those conclusions."[40] Ideological practice in church music leads to an inability to examine
critically current practice and also whatever latent or undeveloped theory that ideological practice is based on.

Second, music affects the life of the church at several vital
points, for example, worship, evangelism, education, and
fellowship, to name some important areas. The general consensus of the church down through the centuries has been
that music has a contribution of its own to make to aspects
of these activities and others. The idea here has been that if
music was missing from these activities with which it has
customarily been associated, these activities would be for
that reason less than satisfactory to the participants involved. If a clear rationale for church music is missing, music's role in these important church actions becomes
uncertain and open to misunderstanding, exploitation, or
abuse. Music may then on occasion be used in such a way
that entire actions of the church may be obscured or displaced, as when the exclusive use of liturgical music ensures

that other uses of music in the church are neutralized. Distorted thinking in church music is bound to impoverish the functioning of the church in one way or another.

Third, without a sound theory for church music, we have no principles with which to transcend our immediate situation and help the church to adapt in times of change and upheaval. Judging from the current problems in Catholic church music discussed before, it appears that the leadership assumed that church music could fall into line with the reforms initiated in other areas without any special preparation. The ensuring confusion in Catholic church music indicates that this probable assumption was a major error. Changes thought to be necessary in one area of the church's life (e.g., worship or the use of vernacular languages instead of Latin) will of necessity ramify throughout other areas. A church music without a strong theory for its practice is not fortified to deal effectively with a situation like this, since it is impossible to decide which of the proposed changes are really essential and which are merely cosmetic.

Fourth, without a theory of church music we are unable to relate church music as a discipline to important theological concerns in a productive way. The practice of church music need not concern itself in a scholarly way with doctrines about the mission of the church, creation, preservation, redemption, Scripture, and the nature of the gospel, for example. Yet if there is no place at all in the discipline of church music for connecting with theological disciplines like systematic theology and theological ethics, church music will continue to produce anemic and superficial music not appropriate to the grandeur and wonder of the Christian faith.

Fifth, the lack of a coherent theory of church music causes major problems as the church moves across cultural and linguistic boundaries to plant itself in more and more ethnic enclaves. Practically based procedures which worked well in

one culture can prove disastrous when uncritically trans-
planted to another culture. Without a theory of church music, one which needs to be cross-culturally applicable, one
cannot achieve the necessary critical distancing from urgent
practical problems so as to devise procedures appropriate to
the new culture. Frequently, even the church sending missionaries finds that it is actually estranged from its own
surrounding musical culture as well. Robert Kauffman, an
ethnomusicologist, has provided a good illustration of this.
He observes that forcing modern Western young people to
participate in a foreign music medium, for example, certain
highly artistic choir anthems, is not unlike "the approach of
early missionaries who insisted that the Christians of India
sing in four-part harmony."[41] While the practice of church
music may not have the objectivity to deal with problems
like this and a host of other culture-related musical difficulties, a theory of church music has the appropriate conceptual
framework within which to view them.

On the basis of these five reasons and the practical problems mentioned earlier, one must conclude that a theory of
church music is definitely needed. My aim in this book is to
outline what such a theory might look like.

Notes

1. Paul Baker, *Contemporary Christian Music* (Westchester: Crossway Books, 1985)
174-181. For a fascinating experiment on "backward masking" see Stephen B.
Thorne and Philip Himelstein, "The Role of Suggestion in the Perception of Satanic
Messages in Rock-and-Roll Recordings," *The Journal of Psychology*, 1984, pp. 116,
245-248.

2. Baker in *Contemporary Christian Music*, has a good survey of many of these
issues.

3. Made during a seminar of the 1986 Gospel Music Association gathering in
Nashville, Tennessee.

3a. Bernard Lonergan has an indispensable discussion on this in his book, *Method
in Theology* (New York: Continuum Press, 1972). He postulates a distinction between

the realm of common sense and the realm of theory, and places history in the realm of common sense. Theology, on this understanding, belongs to the realm of theory. See pp. 81-82,216,230,233,274, and 305.

3b. For the New Testament, see Brevard Childs, *Introduction to the Old Testament as Scripture* (London: SCM Press, 1979) p.78. For the New Testament, see Peter Stuhlmacher, *Historical Criticism and Theological Interpretation of Scripture* (Philadelphia: Fortress Press, 1977) pp. 23-24.

3c. Bernard Lonergan, *Method in Theology*, p.138, my emphasis.

4. Harold Best, "Church Music Curriculum" *Proceedings of the Fifty-Seventh Annual Meeting*, National Association of Schools of Music, (Dallas, Texas, 1982) pp. 137-138.

5. Jay Wilkey, "Prolegomena to a Theology of Music," *Review and Expositor*, Vol. 69, 1972, 507-517, see p.510.

6. Paul Wohlgemuth, *Rethinking Church Music*, rev. ed. (Carol Stream, Ill.: Hope Publishing Company, 1981) p.ix.

7. Peter Jeffery, Review of "Music and Worship in Pagan and Christian Antiquity" by J. Quasten, *Worship*, Vol. 58, No.3, May 1984, 261-263, see p. 261.

8. Lionel Dakers, *Church Music in a Changing World* (London: Mowbray 1984) p. 106.

9. Thom Granger, "Steve Camp: The Grace that Covers Him," *Contemporary Christian Music Magazine*, November 1986, pp. 18-21, see p. 20.

10. J.H. Kwabena Nketia, *The Music of Africa* (New York W.W. Norton and Company, 1974). pp. 14-15.

11. Ethnomusicologist John Blacking has documented this for the Venda people of Southern Africa. See p. 77 of his *How Musical Is Man?* (Seattle: University of Washington Press, 1974). From this diagram you will notice that Western church music is about as far away from the music closest to the hearts of Venda people as it is possible to get.

12. A. M. Jones, *African Hymnody in Christian Worship* (Gwelo: Mambo Press, 1976) p. 34.

13. Heinz Schuster, "Pastoral Theology" *Encyclopedia of Theology* ed. Karl Rahner (New York: The Seabury Press, 1975) pp. 1178-1182, see p. 1182.

14. Carl Schalk, "Thoughts on Smashing Idols: Church Music in the 80s," *The Christian Century*, Sept. 30, 1981, 960-963, see p. 961.

15. Peter Jeffery, Review, 261.

16. Joseph Gelineau, "Music and Singing in the Liturgy" *The Study of Liturgy*, ed. C. Jones, G. Wainwright and E. Yarnold (London: S.P.C.K., 1978) pp. 440-454, see p. 443.

17. Erik Routley, *The Church and Music*, revd. ed. (London: Duckworth, 1967) p. 228.

18. *Ibid.*, p.229.

19. Bruce Leafblad, "What Sound Church Music?" *Christianity Today*, May 19, 1978, 18-20, see p.20.

20. See the recent proposal to reverse this situation by Carlton R. Young, "An Alternative Model for the Education of the Church Musician," *Duty and Delight:*

Routley Remembered ed. R. A. Leaver, J. H. Litton, and Carlton R. Young (Norwich: Canterbury Press, 1985) pp. 97-100.

21. There is a definitive review of all the research on this topic by Paul Wohlgemuth, "Church-Music Education in American Protestant Seminaries," *Duty and Delight: Routley Remembered,* pp. 89-95.

22. Peter Jeffery, Review, p.261.

23. The phrase comes from Donald Hustad's book, *Jublilate! Church Music in the Evangelical Tradition* (Carol Stream, Ill.: Hope Publishing Company, 1981) pp. vii-ix.

24. Paul Wohlgemuth, *Rethinking Church Music,* p.16.

25. David Martin, *A Sociology of English Religion* (London: Heinemann, 1967) p. 86.

26. Erik Routley, *Christian Hymns Observed* (London: Mowbray, 1982) p. 106.

27. Joseph Gelineau, *The Liturgy Today and Tomorrow* (London: Darton, Longman, and Todd, 1978) p. 9.

28. Peter Jeffery, Review, p.261.

29. James F. White, *Christian Worship in Transition* (Nashville: Abingdon Press, 1976) pp. 73-74.

30. Paul Wohlgemuth, *Rethinking Church Music,* p.62.

31. Robert Hayburn, *Papal Legislation on Sacred Music* (Collegeville: The Liturgical Press, 1979) p. 408.

32. Gerard Ebeling, *The Study of Theology* (Philadelphia: Fortress Press, 1978) p. 124.

33. Also see Oskar Söhngen, *Theologische Grundlagen der Kirchenmusik* (Kassel: J. Stauda Verlag, 1967); "What Is the Position of Church Music in Germany Today?" *Cantors at the Crossroads,* e.d. J. Riedel (St. Louis: Concordia, 1967) 201-218; "Music and Theology" *Sacred Sound,* ed. J. Irwin (Chico: Scholars Press, 1983) pp. 1-19.

34. Victor Gebauer, "Theology of Church Music, 20th Century", *Key Words in Church Music,* ed. C. Schalk (St. Louis: Concordia, 1978) pp. 348-351, see p. 351.

35. Jay Wilkey, "Prolegomena," p. 510. Incidentally, we now have a comprehensive bibliography of Routley's publications on pages 243-304 of *Duty and Delight: Routley Remembered.*

36. Four recent contributors have attempted to provide help in this area. I will discuss them very briefly in chronological order. Hustad's *Jubilate!* would seem to provide a theory but it is oriented towards a descriptive, historical and practical perspective. This makes it difficult to derive contemporary norms for church music from it. Johannson's 1984 publication *(Music and Ministry* (Peabody: Hendrickson Publishers, 1984)) is a passionately argued attempt to write a philosophy of church music. He does indeed write one but it is seriously flawed by an adherence to a sociological critique of mass culture which has now been disproved by sociologists. Berglund's *Philosophy of Church Music* (Chicago: Moody Press, 1985) represents the third book in recent years from the Evangelical tradition to attempt a theory of church music. Unfortunately in a 111-page book only 36 pages could be described as philosophical, and even then they do not go far enough. Robin Leaver's brief essay in *Duty and Delight* is more explicitly theological than the other three but still fails, in my opinion, to deal with the fact that music's role in the life of the church is not only restricted to worship. Yet even with these caveats it is exciting that

church musicians are attempting to write a theory of church music. It is a pity that through lack of musical expertise (perhaps) contemporary systematic theologians have allowed themselves to be deterred from attempting this task as well. A recent collection of essays from Roman Catholic musicians and scholars, *Crux et Cithara* (Altötting: Alfred Coppenrath Verlag, 1983) has some interesting points to make but by and large it is disappointing and adds very little to the current need for a theory of church music. I find it disappointing because of the reactionary character of so many of the essays.

37. J. A. Wolfaardt, "Practical Theology," *Practical Theology* (PTH400) ed. J. Symington (Pretoria: University of South Africa, 1980) 98-118, see p. 106.

38. J. A. Wolfaardt, Practical Theology, p. 106.

39. J. S. Kruger, "Theological Ethics," *Introduction to Theology*, 2nd ed., ed. I. H. Eybers, A. Konig and J. A. Stoop (Pretoria: D. R. Church Booksellers, 1978) 199-229, see p. 226.

40. J. A. Wolfaardt, Practical Theology, p. 107.

41. Robert Kauffman, "An Ethnomusicologist Looks at Church Music in the Seventies," *Music Ministry*, 3, Dec. 1970, 2-4, see p. 4.

1

The Christian
and Music Today

Introduction

A Christian is a person to whom it has been revealed that
he or she is a sinner, alienated from God and totally unable
to overcome that alienation. A Christian is a person who
gratefully accepts that in Jesus Christ all sins have been
forgiven and that he or she now stands spotless in the presence of God. A Christian is a person who now lives a new
life by the power of the Holy Spirit and who looks forward
to the second coming of Jesus Christ.

It is clear that such a radical transformation in a human
being's life (however briefly and inadequately I may have
described it) has to result in a new perspective on their lives
and their world. Yet, this is a world which is musical, a
world which loves music and spends a great deal of time and
money making music and listening to music. What does our
Christian faith have to do with music? As with every other
aspect of our lives in this world, the answer is: a great deal.
From a theological point of view we can express it this way:
God is at the center of our existence as Christians, and our
knowledge of Him—or His knowledge of us—now deter-
mines our whole lives. But what is the nature of this God
who knows us and has granted us the privilege of knowing
Him? The Bible reveals the nature of God under many pic-
tures or images, but three seem to have a certain prominence

—God as Creator, Preserver, and Redeemer. These three aspects of God provide three important perspectives from which to examine music. Using these three headings we will consider Music and Creation, Music and Preservation, and Music and Redemption.

Music and Creation

In the very first chapter of the Bible, the third verse, we are given an insight into the nature of God—God makes sounds (He speaks) and these sounds have meaning (that is, God intends to communicate so as to be understood): "And God said, Let there be light." Even before light, there was sound, meaningful sound, sound to which the then uncreated and nonexistent world responded to in an instant: "and there was light" (Gen. 1:3). This verse defines for the rest of Scripture the nature of God; this is a God for whom meaningful sound—in this case speech—is critically important. This is a God who speaks creation into existence, a God who speaks with the intention of being understood, a God who speaks in hope that something and someone in His creation will respond in speech.

Sound at the service of meaning is, therefore, at the heart of the universe. There are two very interesting pieces of information which tend to corroborate the theological significance of ordered sound as portrayed in Genesis 1, one from ancient philosophy, the other from modern physics.

In the sixth century BC the Greek philosopher Pythagoras (according to legend) passed a blacksmith and heard how the hammers produced harmonies. He then discovered from this the basic musical intervals of an octave, fifth and fourth. To his amazement, further research using stretched strings showed that these intervals had precise ratios: two to one for the octave, three to two for the fifth, and four to three for the fourth.[1] In the words of a modern philosopher, Pythagoras had discovered that "the intervals that constitute

the foundations of Western harmony are built into the
world. . . . music is rooted in the nature of things."[2]

Our other confirmation comes from modern physics.
David Bohm has called the underlying reality of the universe "the implicate order." Music, while its notes are still
reverberating in our consciousness, gives us "the sense of a
whole unbroken. . . . In listening to music, one is therefore
directly perceiving an implicate order."[3] As for Phythagoras,
music is the core of the essential nature of created reality.
When we perceive music, we are perceiving the essence of
the universe in a way different from any other art form. It
is significant that a prominent physicist and a famous
philosopher agree that ordered, intelligible sound is built
into the very essence of the physical universe.

But God did not only create sound and through the sound
of His word create the world—He also created mankind—
the only other creature who has the facility of ordering
sound intelligibly so as to hear the Creator speak and to
speak to Him in return. So sound not only constitutes *natural*
reality in its essence, but also *cultural* reality. In Genesis 2:19
we see God asking Adam to name all the creatures He had
formed out of the ground. As the man sounds out the names
of all the creatures God has made, human sound making
constitutes human life or culture. As God spoke the universe
into being, so man speaks the universe of human meanings
into existence. Not only are animals assigned names and
places in mankind's world but also his helper's relationship
to himself is constituted by ordered, intelligible sounds:

> The man said:
> "This is now bone of my bones
>   and flesh of my flesh;
> she shall be called 'woman'
>   for she was taken out of man" (Gen. 2:23).

God is portrayed in the first narrative of creation as concluding that His entire work of creation—including mankind—was very good (Gen 1:31). But this is not an innate goodness. Its goodness consists in its being "good for. . . ." the purposes that God has created for it.[4]

In the second narrative of creation, the trees in the garden are described as "pleasing to the eye and good for food" (Gen 2:9). There is no suggestion that this sensual enjoyment was wrong in any way. The fact that the same features of the tree were part of the series of rationalizations which led Eve to sin against God does not invalidate the judgment of Genesis 2:9 where persons are clearly intended to enjoy what God has created and to enjoy it to the full.[5]

But side by side with this emphasis on creation as a gift for mankind to enjoy is the notion that we are responsible for creation. We are required to rule creation (Gen 1:28), to work the soil, and to take care of the environment (Gen 2:15). Both emphases are positive—there is the enjoyment of God's creation and the happy duty of taking care of it.[6] If by analogy we apply this to sound and music we can conclude that music is good and God gives it to us as a gift to enjoy. It is also evident that as far as the doctrine of creation is concerned, the sounds of nature and culture cannot take care of themselves. Mankind is called to rule sounds, to order them, work them, and take care of them. It is a noble calling to be a musician (at any level) and to embark on the arduous but necessary task of bringing order to the world of sound, so that it produces pleasing sounds to sustain our lives and so fulfill God's call.

Yet already in Genesis 2 we start to get hints that while mankind will have no problem enjoying these gifts, we may indeed have a problem using creation's gifts in a responsible way. Adam and Eve were free to eat from any tree in the garden but there was one from which they might not eat (vv. 16-17). This is another way of saying that freedom entails responsibility. Adam and Eve, however, decided otherwise,

believing that freedom was the power to do anything they
wanted. In the context of Genesis 3 that meant the freedom
to escape the limitations of being a creature. Mankind was
tempted to imagine that he could perceive reality as God
perceived it. In the event, he was given a glimpse of that
("the man has now become like one of of us" v. 22). But he
could never transcend his creatureliness, nor could he forget
that vision of good and evil which God had granted him.
Mankind remained stuck between the two visions. Because
he used his freedom irresponsibly, he lost his freedom to be
responsible.[7]

The consequences of this were and are enormous. Adam
suddenly faced massive alienation from Eve, Eden, and God.
There was no way back to the unambiguous good of the
created order. In theological terms what happened to mankind was that God judged him. Yet the God of the Bible does
not only judge—He is also gracious. The result is that mixed
in with God's acts of judgment are wonderful acts of mercy.[8]
In the words of theologian Hendrikus Berkhof, because of
the dual factor of mankind and sin, "God's relation to the
world becomes an entirely new one. For that we must look
for a second term besides 'creation.' " The term he chose is
preservation.[9] We will use it, too, and discuss how the Christian is to view music since the fall of mankind.

Music and Preservation

By the word *preservation* is meant that activity of God by
which He preserves this world that He loves from the chaos
that has begun to be unleashed in it by humanity's unholy
alliance with the forces of evil since the fall. There are several very important things we need to understand about
preservation.

First, it has only a redemptive intention. That is, God is
only preserving this world because He wants to save it. The
story of the Flood illustrates this graphically. God could

have destroyed every living thing, including Noah. Why didn't He? Genesis 8:21 tells us that God of His own choice, His own mercy, decided He would never again curse the ground because of mankind. Notice that it is not because He decided to turn a blind eye to human wickedness. The very next phrase of this verse goes on to say "even though every inclination of his heart is evil from childhood."

Second, this leads to the observation that in preservation, God does not approve at all of human sin but in fact preserves mankind from God's own righteous judgment. Helmut Thielicke described God's work of preservation as being embodied in certain structures or orders. He called them "the structural form of man's fallen existence." God's response to human sin embodied in these orders is a form of His will which adapts itself and does not withdraw from fallen mankind in rigid self-assertion. Instead it pursues him and "makes itself known to him in a form which takes into account the disrupted possibilities of the fallen world. If it did not do this, the will of God could only mean death for the fallen world."[10]

Third, God's orders of preservation are never given in "pure" form; so that "unavoidably and inevitably in 'order' we encounter 'disorder,' in 'lawfulness' also 'unlawfulness,' not only God's will, but also the evil will of men and the satanic anti-God will."[11] These powers are both heavenly and earthly, divine and human, spiritual and political, invisible and structural, and both good and evil.[12]

An example of an order of preservation instituted by God is that of *culture.* Our own culture (whatever it may be) is a set of meanings and values[13] which we take to be so self-evident that we hardly ever question them. Culture is used by God to restrain human evil and yet culture itself can become "demonized." This happens when people exalt their own culture's values at the expense of all other values. A chilling example of this occurred during the Second World

War in Nazi Germany. Yet even though a culture becomes demonized and is ultimately destroyed, human life is impossible without some sort of order. A new culture, usually not much better than the old one, arises out of the ashes of the previous order.

If culture is a preservational structure instituted by God, then so is music, because music is an integral part of every human culture. Since the fall we can say that music is now used by God to preserve human beings from chaos and destruction,[14] like the rest of human culture. While this may seem like a rather cheerless role for music, we must remember that from a biblical point of view, music is absolutely vital and necessary to human life.

There is an interesting biblical confirmation of this preservational view of music in the first reference to music making in the Bible which comes in a genealogy in Genesis 4:17-26. Genealogies in Genesis have a predominantly theological function.[15] On the surface this particular genealogy appears to be a list of the founders of civilization, but underneath it is clear that "this has been a progress in sin as much as in civilization."[16] Still, despite their shortcomings, the line of Cain did contribute to the development of culture. In this way they inadvertently (from their point of view) fulfilled God's plan that human life be preserved from chaos. Music is a key element in this plan of God embodied in the order of preservation, along with cattle farmers and metalworkers. We, therefore, cannot be "biblical" and at the same time relegate the pursuit of music to the realm of luxuries or an optional extra. Music is a necessity. Here we anticipate certain conclusions from the section on the meaning of music which will explain why music is a necessity. Briefly, it appears that music provides a safe outlet for humanity's aggressive impulses. In this way it preserves us from being more evil than we already are and so, to a limited extent, music cooperates with other preservational structures, to restrain chaos from engulfing humanity.

In addition, the nature of music as gift and task carries over from the order of creation into the order of preservation. God has not withdrawn music as a gift and task from our lives. What has changed, of course, is our ability to handle God's gifts with any degree of responsibility. What normally tends to happen is that under the pressure of human sinfulness, a preservational structure, because it seems to offer some sort of order or stability in a very disordered world, becomes idolized. There is some evidence that this has happened with music for some people in contemporary life. Sociologist David Martin remarks that "The concert is a contemporary high mass for the modern bourgeoisie.... Amongst a large number of people it is taken for granted that music is a theophany"[17] (that is, that music reveals God to us).

This idolizing of music is wrong since it represents a misunderstanding of God's redemptional intention with the structures of preservation, as Hendrikus Berkhof pointed out. Preservational structures "are means not purpose. They must lead us to Christ and become the expression of his love. Failing to do that, they can become idols and make separation between God and us."[18]

In conclusion, one consequence which flows from the decision to see music as a preservational structure (itself part of the larger preservational structure of culture) needs to be discussed.

Biblically speaking, it is necessary to see cultural/linguistic diversity as itself a preservational structure of a higher order than culture itself. This can be illustrated as in figure 1.

That cultural-linguistic diversity is itself a preservational structure can be easily demonstrated from the Bible. After the fall, mankind still retained his gift of language. Yet, as

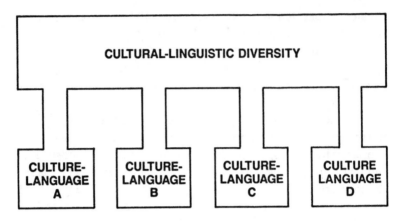

FIGURE 1:
CULTURAL-LINGUISTIC DIVERSITY AS A PRESERVATIONAL STRUCTURE

the results of human alienation from God began to work themselves out, language eventually became the means by which mankind wanted to declare his independence from God. We find the story recorded in Genesis 11:1-9. God confounded human language, making the transcending of human separateness an impossibility apart from Him. Yet all of God's judgments have a redemptive intent. It is only in the New Testament that this intent is made plain. In Paul's sermon in Acts 17, we find Paul saying that even in the division of peoples into linguistic communities (and thereafter inevitably, into cultural groupings, since language is the most important factor in cultural differentiation), God had a supremely gracious purpose: "he determined the times set for them and the exact places where they should live. God did this so that men would seek him and perhaps reach out for him and find him, though he is not far from each one of us" (vv. 26-27). God as Creator decided that humans, no matter how many ways they tried to overcome their alienation from others, would not solve the riddle of their corporateness, their humanity, until they found the New Man,

Jesus Christ. Cultural diversity is then clearly a means by which God preserves us as human beings from our own sinfulness, yet always with a redemptive intention.

But, you may be saying, didn't God overcome and remove these barriers dividing people on the Day of Pentecost? Many scholars interpret these verses as a reversal of Babel, but I think the biblical evidence points in the other direction. In the words of biblical scholar R. C. H. Lenski, "The diversity of languages has continued unchanged. Even Greek, a world language, did not endure."[19] Luke's listing of all the geographical and cultural regions represented on the Day of Pentecost (Acts 2:9-11) suggests that the gospel was intended for all nations and all languages. It was in no way a reversal of Babel. It was rather a continuation of the preservational structure of cultural diversity into the age of the Spirit. The Holy Spirit would now assist and insist on the church speaking the gospel so that each one would hear it in their own native language (v. 8).

What has this to do with music? Simply this: musical diversity is as much the will of God in the order of preservation as is cultural and linguistic diversity. This means that *no* musical style is superior or inferior to any other musical style, just as *no* language or culture is superior or inferior to any other language or culture. Since there is so much conflict between Christians today on the issue of musical taste this point needs to be reiterated: every style of music in the world is valid and has a place in God's order of preservation. (I will have more to say about this contentious issue in the section on the meaning of music.)

I have made the point several times that God's purpose in establishing the order of preservation was redemptive in intent. We are now in a position to examine music's role in that order of redemption.

Music and Redemption

While the preservational mode of God's involvement with the world refers to His implicit and indirect restraint of evil in this world, in the redemptional mode God becomes explicit and direct. He says clearly and unambiguously that He desires to overcome mankind's alienation from Himself and has instituted a new order especially for this purpose. In the process He creates the possibility for mankind to be both genuinely free and responsible. The order of redemption has two distinct phases, the Old Testament and the New Testament. We will consider them in this order, although they represent one unified redemptive order.

1. The Old Testament Order of Redemption and Music

The formal, explicit history of salvation or redemption begins with the call of Abraham and progresses through the long history of the Jewish people till the coming of Christ. From this history, can one learn anything distinctive for a theological evaluation of music?

When we examine the references to music in the Bible, we find that "music pervaded every aspect of life in the Old Testament".[20]

As far as the relationship between music and the supernatural is concerned, we find that music was used to drive away evil spirits (1 Sam 16:16,23); to dispose one for possession by a supernatural force (2 Kings 3:15); as a part of the sacrificial ritual in the Temple (2 Chron. 23:18); and, above all, for praying to and praising God (the Book of Psalms). This by no means exhausts the uses of music in the Bible,[21] but one looks in vain for any distinctive theological ideas about music in the Old Testament. This is all the more surprising when one considers their creativity in matters theological and religious. In point of fact, it appears that the Israelite attitude to music was no different from its non-

Israelite neighbors. For example, the area central to the performance of religious music, namely, the Temple, was built by the Phoenicians. The only difference between the Jewish Temple and Phoenician temples was that the Jewish Temple did not contain an image of the Deity. Other than that, the descriptions of Solomon's Temple given in the Bible "match the things discovered in Phoenician temples."[22] Von Rad noted that "in the matter of her sacred song, Israel went to school with the Canaanites. The idea is even entertained that she took over whole poems from the Canaanite cult."[23] This meant that there was "nothing unique about the Psalms as a literary, religious form."[24] As careful a scholar as Roland de Vaux, using the lists of singers in 1 Kings 5:11, came to the conclusion that it is "not too bold to think that the first choir of singers for the Temple at Jerusalem was recruited from among non-Israelites."[25] Sigmund Mowinckel concluded bluntly: "Beyond all doubt the temple singing in Israel can be traced back to Canaanite patterns."[26]

The net result of these historical facts and probabilities is that Israel simply followed, in all likelihood, the same uses and styles of music as her neighbors.[27] There is, then, no evidence anywhere in the Old Testament or deuterocanonicals of a use of music which could be called distinctively "biblical," a use of music which could not be easily paralleled among Israel's neighbors. In a situation like this, it is sometimes just as important to establish what the Scriptures do not say, as it is to find out what they do say. However, this does not mean a purely negative result. The fact that Israel used the music available to it from its own populace and neighbors without a qualm (so far as we can tell), must mean that the musical product as product is not an area where theological or religious criticism is thought to be important. An illustration of this can be found in Amos 5:23-24;6:5. Significantly, all of these references are to the moral and religious failures of music producers and music inter-

preters—not the musical product. What we must conclude
from this is that there is no style of music which was distinctively "biblical." The Old Testament is indifferent to such
matters. The Old Testament, in other words, is more inter-
ested in the music maker than the style of music made.

Although the history of Israel may not provide any positive revelation about music, there is one more fact about the
Old Testament which is significant. Samuel Terrien, in his
recent attempt at writing a biblical theology which does
justice to both Old and New Testaments, has emphasized
the concept of presence as a unifying thread in the
heterogeneity of the biblical documents: "The motif of presence induces a magnetic field of forces which maintains a
dynamic tension, in the whole of scripture, between divine
self-disclosure and divine self-concealment."[28] Following
this motif through the Scriptures, Terrien came upon a secondary motif: that the biblical writers in general tended to
favor the ear over the eye as the organ of revelation.[29] The
relevance of this for an understanding of the role of music
in the Old Testament era is that of all the communication
arts, music would of necessity receive the greatest impetus
next to speech in a religion where the ear was favored over
the eye.

This is in fact what happened, according to Claus Westermann. He affirmed that music always had great significance
for Israel because "it was so close to human speech and
because art was all but identical with the art of speech and
sound."[30] Since the behavior which God required was not
visibly communicated—it demanded the hearing and the
obeying of God's word—vocal music would therefore have
played a critically important role in the process of revelation
and response we find described in the pages of the Old
Testament. This also included (although in a secondary,
supportive role) instruments in the Old Testament, where
they function as signs that nonhuman creation is also called

to praise God. Instruments made from reed, hide, gut, pottery, bone, ivory, and metals[31] represent the earth raised in the worship of God: "Shout for joy to the Lord, all the earth, . . . make music to the Lord with the harp" (Ps. 98:4-5a).[32]

2. The New Testament Order of Redemption and Music

The New Testament exhibits the same indifference to music as the Old Testament, with a few exceptions. That is not so say that music was unimportant to their lives—just that there are no guidelines laid down as to the "right" sort of music to listen to or sing, apart from the extremely broad statements of Paul in Philippians 4:8. Hymnologist Louis Benson, has some wonderful insights on this point and they are worth quoting in full:

> At the Last Supper the company would use [the tune] they associated with the Hallel. Our Lord had no intent of imposing upon his church his national music or ritual. The particular tune they used did not become an oral tradition, and could not have been made a part of the written gospel, since no system of notation had been invented. I have often thought how happy that circumstance was. If the music had been included in the narrative, as it would be in a modern phonographic record, it would inevitably have acquired a sacrosanct character. It might have formed the basis of a system of church music that would have kept the later church outside the development of modern culture. . . . our Lord imposed no type of music upon his church.[33]

Yet, although neither Jesus nor the apostles imposed any particular style of music as innately "sacred," the impact of the gospel on our world means that our evaluation of everything, including music has changed. In the life, death, and resurrection of Christ all things, meaning the totality of created reality, have been made new: "If anyone is in Christ, he is a new creation; the old has gone, the new has come!" (2 Cor. 5:17). This not only includes individuals, but also the entire cosmos: "Through him to reconcile to himself all things, whether things on earth or things in heaven, by making peace through his blood, shed on the cross" (Col. 1:20).

One vitally important thing to notice about this saving work of Christ is that although it is an eternal work, for us on this side of eternity, we have to experience it in terms of our own time framework. This means that the first coming of Christ inaugurated the final phase of the order of redemption, but it is only the second coming of Christ which will signal its consummation. Those who have responded to the gospel message of forgiveness for sin live quite literally between two times, two ages, two worlds—the world to come, the kingdom of God which is inexorably pressing its massive weight into our space and time, and the kingdom of this world, ruled by Satan with the full consent of mankind in rebellion against God. Make no mistake about it: Christ has conquered the kingdom of this world (John 16:33) and all authority is now in His hands (Matt. 28:18). Yet this victory has to work itself out in our time framework of history. When that has been done to God's satisfaction, history and our world will end in time as certainly as it had a beginning in time. In the meantime we are in this world but not of it (John 17:14-18).

What this means as far as music is concerned is as follows. The orders of creation and preservation continue to exist with their features, although they have now been completely transcended by the order of redemption. Transcended, but not destroyed. Music is still a gift to enjoy and a responsibility under the order of creation. It is a means of preserving our lives under the order of preservation and we must gratefully accept it as such. The order of redemption points beyond everything this world has to offer—both good and bad—and says that Christ has made all things new. In that new world, our lives will be so radically transformed that even music will be unnecessary. But there is another point about music in the order of redemption which is important.

In this present time, caught between the demise of the old world and the birth pangs of the new world, as we are, music has a special function in the order of redemption: the communication of the good news that our sins have been forgiven in Christ. Music in the order of redemption now becomes the handmaid of the church in its ceaseless task of communicating the gospel. Paul put it very clearly and his text forms the basis for our considerations on the role of music in the church later in this book: "Let the word of Christ dwell in you richly as you teach and admonish one another with all wisdom, and as you sing psalms, hymns and spiritual songs with gratitude in your heart to God" (Col 3:16).

Before we conclude this section on the Christian and music today, I would like to summarize the role of music in the three orders of creation, preservation, and redemption. Figure 2 provides a rapid overview of this.

The task of the Christian today, as will be seen from the diagram, is to give music its due in all three orders. Music's role in all three still stands and demands our active involvement. When we emphasize music's role in one order, it is usually at the expense of its role in other orders and an imbalance results. This happens, for example, when people so emphasize the creational status of music as a gift that they may downplay its role as a task given to mankind. Some even forget entirely that the fall occurred, that we are now living under the order of preservation and that music in this age is made by fallen human beings. If we can remember which aspect of music we are discussing at which point, it will go a long way to helping us become clearer as to music's role in our lives from a Christian point of view.

Yet while we have talked about the *role* of music in our lives, we have not been specific as to its *meaning* in our lives. What does music mean? Does music have a meaning? If it

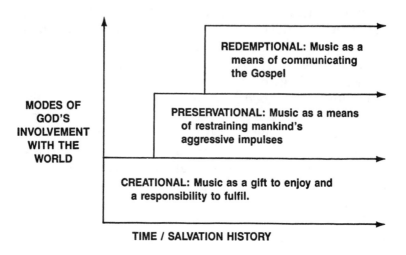

REDEMPTIONAL: Music as a
means of communicating
the Gospel

MODES OF
GOD'S
INVOLVEMENT
WITH THE
WORLD

PRESERVATIONAL: Music as a means
of restraining mankind's
aggressive impulses

CREATIONAL: Music as a gift to enjoy and
a responsibility to fulfil.

TIME / SALVATION HISTORY

FIGURE 2:
MUSIC'S ROLE IN THE ORDERS OF CREATION, PRESERVATION
AND REDEMPTION

does, what is that meaning? We need to attempt to answer
such questions if we are to have a clear understanding of
music's place in our lives and our world today. Unfortunately, the Bible is not a textbook on musical aesthetics and does
not provide us with answers to these particular questions.
This means that we will have to go outside the Bible and
grapple with some of the issues about the meaning of music
currently being discussed by philosophers, musicologists,
and other scholars. We will not arrive at a definitive answer
to the question of what music means, but I believe there is
enough of a consensus to shed some light on this question.
Once we have done this we will be in a position to embark
on the second section of our discussion: how our Christian
faith relates to the music of the church today. The question
as to the role of music in the church cannot be adequately
answered, in my opinion, until we have first developed a
perspective on the role of music in our culture and its mean-

ing. So it is to the question of the meaning of music that we now turn.

Notes

1. I am using the account of this given by Oskar Söhngen, "Music and Theology: A Systematic Approach," in *Sacred Sound*, ed. Joyce Irwin (Chicago: Scholars Press, 1983) pp.1-19.

2. Bryan Magee, *The Philosophy of Schopenhauer* (Oxford: Clarendon Press, 1983) p.187.

3. I am indebted to Michael Rubinstein for this reference. It comes from his fascinating book on musical taste, *Music to My Ear* (London: Quartet Books, 1985) pp.182-184.

4. Claus Westermann, *Genesis 1-11: A Commentary* (Minneapolis: Augsburg Publishing House, 1984) p.166.

5. Westermann, p.249: "The desire of the sense is part of God's gift."

6. Helmut Thielicke, *Theological Ethics: Foundations* (Grand Rapids: Wm. B. Eerdmans, 1966) p.152. Here Thielicke defines the image of God as both gift and task, "the task implicit in the gift."

7. Helmut Thielicke, *Theological Ethics*, p.281. See also p.284: "Thus the final act of man's originally unbroken freedom is that in which freedom destroys itself."

8. Gerhard von Rad, *Old Testament Theology: Volume 1.* (Edinburgh: Oliver and Boyd, 1962) 163. Here Von Rad comments on Genesis 1-11: "God punished these outbreaks of sin with increasingly severe judgments. Nevertheless, there is also to be seen, mysteriously associated with this punishment, a saving and sustaining activity on the part of God which accompanied man. God no doubt banished the first pair from the garden. But he clothed them, and after all allowed them to remain alive."

9. Hendrikus Berkhof, *Christian Faith* (Grand Rapids: Wm. B. Eerdmans, 1978) p.211.

10. Helmut Thielicke, *Theological Ethics*, p.148, see especially pp.434-451.

11. W. Künneth, "The Concept of the Order of Preservation" in *Faith and Action*, ed. H.H. Schrey (Edinburgh: Oliver and Boyd, 1970) pp.282-292. This quotation is from p. 291. The entire article is perhaps the clearest statement on the doctrine of preservation currently available.

12. This concept comes from Walter Wink's invaluable study, *Naming the Powers* (Philadelphia: Fortress Press, 1984) p.100.

13. The definition is from Bernard Lonergan's superb book, *Method in Theology* (New York: The Seabury Press, 1972) p.301.

14. This assessment of music's role since the fall is confirmed by the great German writer on the theology of music, Oskar Söhngen. He writes: "Music belongs to the *bonae ordinationes Dei*, the gracious creational and preservational orders

by which God maintains this fallen world in his mercy" (my translation). This quotation is from page 208 in his *Theologische Grundlagen der Kirchenmusik* (Kassel: J. Stauda Verlag, 1967).

15. Brevard S. Childs, *Introduction to the Old Testament as Scripture* (London: SCM Press, 1979) pp.152-152.

16. Clines, David J. A., *The Theme of the Pentateuch* (Sheffield: JSOT Press, 1978) p.67.

17. David Martin, *The Breaking of the Image* (Oxford: Basil Blackwell, 1980) pp.141-142.

18. Hendrikus Berkhof, *Christian Faith*, p.214.

19. R. C. H. Lenski, *The Interpretation of the Acts of the Apostles* (Minneapolis: Augsburg Publishing House, 1934) p.62.

20. K. M. Campbell, "The Role of Music in Worship", *The Evangelical Quarterly*, Vol. LII, No 1. Jan-Mar 1980, pp.43-46. Quotation is from p. 43.

21. Eric Werner, "Music," *Interpreter's Dictionary of the Bible*, Vol. III, ed. G. Buttrick (Nashville: Abingdon Press, 1962). See also his article, "Jewish Music," *The New Grove Dictionary of Music and Musicians*, Vol 12, ed. S. Sadie (London: Macmillan, 1980) pp.614-634.

22. John H. Tullock, *The Old Testament Story* (Englewood Cliffs, pp. N.J.: Prentice-Hall 1981) p.169.

23. Gerhard von Rad, *Old Testament Theology*, Vol. 1, p.24.

24. Michael Ball, *Singing to the Lord* (London: Bible Reading Fellowship, 1979) p.8.

25. Roland de Vaux, *Ancient Israel, Its Life and Institutions* (London: Darton, Longman, and Todd, 1961) p.382.

26. Sigmund Mowinckel, *The Psalms in Israel's Worship,* Vol. III (Oxford: Basil Blackwell, 1962) p.81.

27. Musicological confirmation of this can be found in Alfred Sendrey, *Music in Ancient Israel* (New York: Philosophical Library, 1969) 59, and in Abraham Schwadron, "On Jewish Music" in *Musics of Many Cultures*, ed. E. May (Berkeley: University of California Press, 1980) pp.284-306, page 286.

28. Samual Terrien, *The Elusive Presence* (New York: Harper and Row, 1978) p.43.

29. Samuel Terrien, *The Elusive Presence*, pp.70, 146, 201-202, 268, 279, 431, 436.

30. Claus Westermann, *Genesis 1-11*, p.332,

31. Bathja Bayer, "The Finds that Could not Be," *Biblical Archaelogy Review*, Vol VIII, No. 1, Jan/Feb 1982, pp.20-36, see p.22

32. See the discussion on this in Pierre Casetti, "Funktionen der Musik in der Bibel," *Freiburger Zeitschrift für Philosophie und Theologie*, Vol. 24, 1977, pp.366-389.

33. Louis F. Benson, *The Hymnody of the Christian Church* (Philadelphia: Westminister Press, 1927) pp.233-234.

2

The Meaning of Music

As a useful starting point for our discussion, I would like
to propose two models: one of the musical event, the other
of musical meaning.

A Model of the Musical Event

Music does not happen in the abstract. It usually occurs
as a definite event. To help us understand what happens in
this event, musicologist Jean-Jacques Nattiez has developed
a model of the musical event which we will use and later
modify in a model of church music. He calls it "The functional tripartition of music" and what it looks like can be
seen in figure 3.

As we look at Nattiez's model, we see that there are three
components—a producer, an artifact, and an interpreter. The
producer is the one who "makes" the music—either as a com-
poser, an improviser (as in jazz), or as a performer. Without
the producer, music does not exist. Looking at the other end
of the diagram we see the interpreter. The *interpreter* is the
person who hears the music produced by the producer.
Sometimes the producer and the interpreter may be one and
the same person, as when a person sings or plays for himself
or herself. Most times, though, the producer makes music
for a group, in either a live situation or by means of a
recording. The means by which the producer and the interpreter are linked into one network of communication is the

41

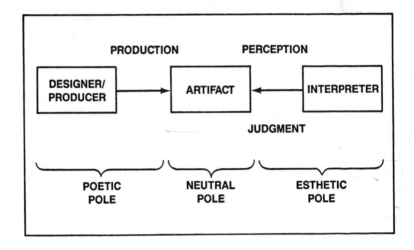

FIGURE 3:
THE FUNCTIONAL TRIPARTITION OF MUSIC[1]

artifact (i.e., the music as a sequence of sounds which begin in time and end in time).

The most important thing this model helps us to do with regard to music is to see that the meanings of a piece of music are exchanged between producer and interpreter through the artifact. To put it another way, the artifact, the music, doesn't *intend* anything or mean anything by itself. The *people* who produce the music and the people who interpret the music intend and find meanings in it. Linguists are fond of saying that meanings are not in words—they are in your head. Take for instance the word *die*. Depending on the context it could mean to cease existence or a machine. The meaning is not "in" the word—the meaning is "in" our heads. The exact same process occurs when we make or listen to music. We are continuously reading meanings into the music for the duration of the musical event and sometimes longer. We could not intend those meanings without that particular musical piece being played or sung. In other words, that particular artifact has to exist for us to intend those meanings, but the meanings intended are entirely under *our* control and not the music's.[2]

This particular understanding of music has an impressive confirmation in the New Testament. In Mark 7, Jesus is involved in a running battle with the Pharisees over traditional ideas concerning "clean" and "unclean" hands. Jesus rejects this emphasis on outward ritual cleanliness and emphasizes that it is the inner intention of the man that pollutes him:

> What comes out of a man is what makes him "unclean." For from within, out of men's hearts, come evil thoughts, sexual immorality, theft, murder, adultery, greed, malice, deceit, lewdness, envy, slander, arrogance and folly. All these evils come from inside and make a man "unclean" (vv. 20-23).

Jesus was always getting to the heart of the matter, as it were, emphasizing meaning and intention above external criteria. It is the same with music. It is the intentions of the producer and the interpreter that determine the meaning of the music, not the music. If the meaning you intend in a certain piece of music does not enhance your Christian faith, it is wrong for you to continually expose yourself to that music. If, on the other hand, you do not see harmful meanings in the music, it is emphatically not wrong for you.

Paul encountered the same problem with fastidious Jewish converts to Christianity in the early church. They were plagued by guilt over eating meat offered to idols. Paul, while he respected their scruples, stated that he was fully convinced that no food is unclean in itself. He continued: "But if anyone regards something as unclean, then for him it is unclean" (Rom 14:14). The same basic idea, namely, that the created order is good and that problems originate from within man rather than outside of man, can be found in Titus 1:15: "To the pure, all things are pure, but to those who are corrupted and do not believe, nothing is pure" and in 1 Timothy 4:4-5: "Everything God created is good, and nothing is to be rejected if it is received with thanksgiving, because it is consecrated by the word of God and prayer."

When we see a rock star mouthing obscenities and profanities in a song at a concert, it is difficult for us to separate the musical form from the particular use being made of it at that moment. Yet, if we have the faith to believe it, even that musical style is good and can be used by God at an appropriate time. An abuse of a form by one person does not invalidate use of that form by others.

If the history of church music can teach us one lesson it is that the church has generally been far too slow in adopting newer musical forms to communicate the gospel. Once we can accept that meaning is in our heads and not in the music, all musical styles become available for communicating the gospel. In addition, as discussed earlier, because no culture is inferior to another, neither is any musical style inferior to any other musical style. God in fact has made musical diversity part of his order of preservation. We do not exult in this diversity because we know that it originated in man's sin, but we acknowledge it and work within it, without being absorbed into it.[3]

An outstanding illustration that God can and does use all musical styles to communicate the gospel came to my attention recently in a book by Paul Baker on contemporary Christian music. It concerns a guitarist for an "infamous raunch rock group" who became a Christian. For three years he reacted totally against rock music of any kind and settled down to communicating the gospel in nonrock music. Sometime later he was invited to play for a group of young people, some of whom were drug addicts. They did not like his nonrock music and as they started to walk out of the concert,

Harvey prayed: "I'm just standing there, thinking, 'God, what did I do?' and he spoke to me, saying, 'If you do it for my glory, and not to glorify yourself, I don't mind if you play your guitar'." Harvey went on to play rock music and his audience returned to hear the message of the gospel.[4] Was the musical form any different before this experience than it was afterwards? No, but what a difference in the intention of the performer, and that was what God chose to use.

Before I conclude this discussion on musical meaning, I want to suggest why we respond to musical styles the way we do.

A mass of recent sociological research on musical taste suggests what we know intuitively: Our own life history is the strongest determining factor in the kind of music we like and the kind we don't like.[5] There would be very little problem if we simply stated what kinds of music we liked and what kinds we didn't like. Some of us however go a little further than that, especially in religious circles. We tend to equate a certain musical style with a certain morality and then pass off our aesthetic judgments as moral judgments. This of course has gone on for centuries. Sociologist Howard Becker remarked that:

> People do not experience their aesthetic beliefs as merely arbitrary and conventional; they feel that they are natural, proper and moral. An attack on a convention and an aesthetic is also an attack on a morality. The regularity with which audiences greet major changes in dramatic, musical and visual conventions with vituperative hostility indicates the close relation between aesthetic and moral belief.[6]

Why is this so? Why do we instinctively feel that a certain style of musical is immoral whereas another is moral? David Swanger studied the process of making moral judgments as compared with making aesthetic judgments and found that there are important *parallels* between judging moral issues and judging works of art. Although the processes may be similar, morality and art are not *identical*.[7] It appears as though some people in the church have not only fused morality indiscriminately with art but have in addition claimed religious or ultimate sanction for their favorite musical styles. As recently as 1984 one finds books on church music in which the unfortunate assertion is made that "pop music is alien to the gospel"; that to use pop music as a medium for the gospel message is wrong because "the music has inherently those characteristics that are contrary to what the words mean."[8] Following on from our previous discussion we can see that no meaning is inherently "in" any music unless it has first been put there by human beings. In addition, to say that a style of music is alien to the gospel is the twentieth-century equivalent of refusing to eat meat offered to idols. Just because a form has been abused and associated with sub-Christian and antichristian influences does not mean that the form is invalid.

We have seen in this section *how* the process of musical communication operates. Now we have the delicate and difficult task of suggesting *why* music is so important to us as human beings.

A Model of Musical Meaning

This model of musical meaning is based on a theory of human perception, will, and emotion. It starts with the mind and asserts that our mind interprets reality for us. Our will then responds to that interpretation. The response to that cognitive input from the mind is instanteously fused with the volitional input from the will and the result is an emotion. The diagram in figure 4 illustrates this model of human perception and response.

This is the theory in its concise form.[9] We now need to look at each of its components in more detail.

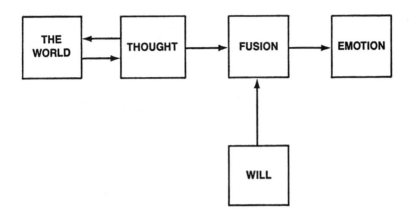

FIGURE 4:
A MODEL OF HUMAN THOUGHT, WILL AND EMOTION

Our *thoughts* are the means by which we interpret reality or, more simply, events. We constantly scan our situation for clues as to the meaning of events and their possible impact on the self.

The *will* is constantly trying to establish, based on input from the mind, whether the self is adequate to a situation as interpreted, or inadequate in that particular situation. The will generates a response.

The will's response can be thought of as a flow of energy which assumes a certain pattern, configuration, or shape. This configuration will last as long as the self believes it necessary to maintain a certain posture of the will. In every-day language we hint at this feature of the will when we say "Well, maybe that will break his will," when speaking, for instance, of a defiant child having just been disciplined. Obviously, no one has ever seen or will ever see "the will," and it is pure metaphor to describe the will as assuming a certain shape. Yet we intend to refer, however inadequately, to a reality of human existence which we know subjectively to be true. If the will's response to a thought can be imagined as a shape sustained by a flow of energy, a pulsating configuration, it is reasonable to see it in three dimensions: that of direction (up or down); duration (long or short); and emphasis (heavy or light). As Roger Scruton has said of one of these dimensions, "At a deep level, the sense of 'up' and 'down' is a sense of the human will."[10]

An *emotion*, as is evident from the diagram, results from the instanteous fusion of the cognitive input from the mind with the volitional response-shape generated by the will. It is therefore an amalgam of cognitive and volitional elements which the self responds to as a sign of its adequacy or inadequacy at that particular moment. For example, when a person says "I am really anxious about taking this exam," what they are saying is the following: I don't perceive myself (thought) to be able to cope (will) with this situation. I therefore generate a response of anxiety (emotion) which is a fusion of my interpretation of the situation (thought) and my response for my perceived ability or inability in that situation (will). The emotion is a sign to myself that I have doubts about my adequacy in that situation. The emotion is a unique fusion of cognitive and volitional elements.

I have now outlined this theory. Does it have anything to do with the meaning of music? I believe it does, in the following way. Music provides an exquisite variety of shapes in which the will can directly relate in exactly those dimensions it is familiar with: up and down, long and short, heavy and light. Music provides an ideal situation (since it is a "protected" situation) where the sole aim is to let the will play endlessly in this paradise of will-shaped configurations: ups, downs, longs, shorts, slows, fasts, louds, softs, and a million points in between! We can use the duration of tone as a sign to ourselves at a deep level that we will endure, our identity will survive. We can use the up and down of tone as a sign to ourselves of the will's adequacy and inadequacy in facing obstacles. We can use louds and softs, longs and shorts, fasts and slows in music as a sign system indicating the inner state of our selves, our wills. In short, in a situation where music is used, we give ourselves permission to rehearse key features of the will's configurations in a situation remote from the "real" world. That rehearsal of the will's response-shapes is critically important to our sense of selfhood as human beings. In his discussion on the human will, Peter Rohner highlighted the centrality of will to identity:

> When man wills something, he seems to exist in a specially active way and to be determined by the personal ego itself. ... In contrast to other modes of existence, when man wills he does not find himself under alien domination but as master of himself ... the act of willing can be called centrifugal. It flows outwards rather than inwards and is determined by the person himself.[11]

The exercise of the will, both in "real" life and in psychically protected situations (as in musical events), is at the core of our identity. This can perhaps explain the importance of music to millions of healthy human beings for centuries and its significance as a tool for psychotherapeutic intervention as in music therapy. We allow music to affect us, unlike other art forms, at the deepest core of our beings— our will. This understanding of the meaning of music helps us to see that music does belong to the order of preservation. This is because music enables us to deal with many aspects of our wills which, if enacted literally in "real" life, would cause untold destruction and misery. Music enables us to work through basic issues of our selfhood at a deep prereflective level and is therefore essential to our lives.

We now need to see how this model of musical meaning relates to the two main opinions as to the meaning of music among philosophers. One opinion says that music's meaning is intrinsic, that is, music's meaning is limited purely to the interplay of sounds perceived. The other school of thought maintains that music's meaning is extrinsic, that is, its meaning has reference to something outside of the music.[12] It would seem that both viewpoints are true, since at times music impresses us with its intramusical meanings, at other times with extramusical meanings. The process of musical perception probably alternates easily between these two poles of musical meaning. If we adapt this to the model sketched below, we get a model of musical meaning (see fig. 5).

Although I have separated the two aspects of musical meaning for convenience they are in reality inseparable.[13]

An example of intramusical meaning would be if I was listening to a certain chord progression which made a surprising modulation. My mind would define it as an unusual modulation, my will would respond to that interpretation with a certain configuration appropriate to the self's cogni-

EXTRA / INTRAMUSICAL MEANING

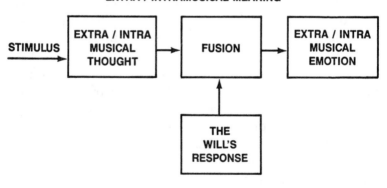

FIGURE 5:
A MODEL OF MUSICAL MEANING

tive interpretation of "surprise." The fusion of the two produces in me an intramusical emotion tied precisely to that particular modulation, such as surprise or some similar emotion.

An example of extramusical meaning would be if I was singing a certain hymn in church and my mind through association was suddenly flooded with memories of times when I was a child in church, the security of being a child in our family, the memory of deep experiences with God. In response to these cognitive images my will produces in response a rapid number of configurations. These fuse instanteously with the memories, and then feelings of nostalgia and longing flood my being.

At certain musical events, one pole may dominate almost to the exclusion of the other. If it is music with which I have few extramusical associations, the meanings I perceive may be largely intramusical. If on the other hand it is a work with which I have a large number of extramusical associations, these may predominate. For example, if I am very familiar with Handel's *Messiah* largely through extramusical meanings, I may spend the whole performance reflecting on these. For a large number of people the extramusical meanings of the "Hallelujah Chorus" would be so overwhelming that at that moment intramusical meanings recede into the background.

Music therefore according to this model of musical meaning becomes meaningful for me as I perceive analogies between the shape of the music and the cognitive interpretation with which the configuration of the will fuses to produce an emotion either extra or intramusical. Notice that both intra and extramusical meanings of music are compatible with the model of musical meaning proposed, because the will's response-shape will be similar since its response is volitionally determined rather than cognitively determined. This is the reason why the same text can be set

to an infinite variety of tunes, a fact universally acknowl-
edged by musicologists and aestheticians.[14]

What is the relevance to the Christian of these assertions
about how musical meaning is communicated and what
music means to us? In a general sense music is necessary to
preserve human beings from the chaos which would engulf
us all if human impulses of the will were not moderated. In
a specifically Christian sense, music combined with words
which reflect valid interpretations of the Christian faith
plays a crucial role in our spiritual growth. This is because
the fusion of cognitive (doctrinal) elements with volitional
elements to produce an emotion happens in a remarkably
effective way through music. That is why it is commonly
said that people learn more theology through music than
they do through sermons. But it is not only cognitive—it is
volitional and emotive at the same time. Christian song, as
Don Saliers has put it, is not simply dressing out words in
sound, rather, "we are engaged in forming and expressing
those emotions which constitute the very Christian life itself."[15] I would not go as far as Saliers and say that these
emotions *constitute* the Christian life—that life can only be
constituted by Christ Himself living in me (Gal 2:20). But I
believe it would be correct to say that the *nurturing* of these
emotions through Christian song is the logical and inevita-
ble result of a life constituted by Christ. With this, we are
now ready to consider what our Christian faith has to do
with the music we use in the community of faith, with
church music as such.

Notes

1. The particular version of Nattiez's typology of the musical event I am using
comes from Otto Laske's stimulating book, *Music, Memory and Thought* (Ann Arbor:
University Microfilms, 1977) p.89.

2. I am indebted to Morse Peckham for first making "the meaning of meaning"

plain to me in his brilliant but largely unknown book, *Explanation and Power* (New York: Seabury Press, 1979).

3. This idea comes from Oscar Cullman, *Salvation in History* (London: SCM Press, 1967) p.335.

4. Paul Baker, *Contemporary Christian Music* (Westchester, N.Y.: Crossway Books, 1985) p.181.

5. Some of the best books and articles on this topic include (in alphabetical order): Judith R. Blau, "High Culture as Mass Culture," *Society*, Vol. 23, No. 4, May-June, 1986, pp.65-69; John Booth Davies, *The Psychology of Music* (Stanford: Stanford University Press, 1978); R. Serge Denisoff, "Massification and Popular Music: A Review," *Journal of Popular Culture*, Vol. 9, No. 4, Spring 1976, pp. 886-894; R. Serge Denisoff, *Solid Gold: The Popular Record Industry* (New Brunswick: Transaction Books, 1975); Jonathan D. Drury, "Modern Popular Music and the South African Challenge," *South African Journal of Musicology*, 5, 1985, pp.7-29; K. Peter Etzkorn, "Manufacturing Music," *Society*, November-December, 1976, pp.19-23; William S. Fox and Michael Wince, "Musical Taste Cultures and Taste Publics," *Youth and Society*, Vol 7, No 2, December 1975, pp.198-224; Herbert J. Gans, *Popular Culture and High Culture* (New York: Basic Books, 1974); George H. Lewis, "Taste Cultures and Culture Classes in Mass Society," *International Review of Aesthetics and Sociology of Music*, Vol 8, No 1, 1977, pp.39-48; also, "Cultural Socialization and the Development of Taste Cultures and Culture Classes in American Popular Music," *Popular Music and Society*, Vol. 4, No 4, 1976, pp.226-241; Robert Irwin Mellem, "Definitions Comprising a Concept Analysis and Theoretical Model of "Good Musical Taste," Unpublished Ed. D. dissertation, Columbia University, 1974; Richard A. Peterson and Paul Di Maggio, "From Region to Class: The Changing Locus of Country Music: A Test of the Massification Hypothesis," *Social Forces*, March 1975, Vol. 53, No. 3, pp.497-506. There are numerous other books and articles but those listed here will give the reader a basic orientation to a body of research which appears largely unknown to church musicians, much to their loss.

6. Howard S. Becker, "Art as Collective Action," *American Sociological Review*, Vol. 36, No. 6, 1974, pp.767-776. See also his *Artworlds* (Berkeley: University of California Press, 1982).

7. David Swanger, "Parallels Between Moral and Aesthetic Judging, Moral and Aesthetic Education," *Educational Theory*, Vol. 35, No 1, Winter 1985, pp.85-96.

8. The reference here is to Calvin Johansson's *Music and Ministry* (Peabody: Hendrickson Publishers, 1984) pp.59, 55. Similar sentiments are found in Robert D. Berglund's book, *A Philosophy of Church Music* (Chicago: Moody Press, 1985) pp.22-36. My rejection of their positions must not be seen as a rejection of them as people. Both are members of the body of Christ, as I am, and I deeply appreciate the effort they have made to write theologies or philosophies of church music.

9. I am not making any great claims for this model and I realise fully its highly speculative nature. However there are pieces of evidence, which, if one were to assemble them in the way I have, to "solve" (if possible) the problem of musical meaning, would probably produce a model similar to mine. The *psychological* support for this model (aspects of it) can be found in David B. Burns' book, *Feeling Good:*

The New Mood Therapy (New York: William Morrow, 1980). His theory is based on cognitive therapy, which, as Burns interprets it, says that our emotions depend on how we interpret events. Frequently negative emotions derive from faulty or unrealistic perceptions of reality. The *philosophical* support (again for aspects of the model only) can be found in Roger Scruton, *The Aesthetic Understanding* (London: Methuen, 1983) and Morse Peckham's magnificent books, *Beyond the Tragic Vision* (New York: Cambridge University Press, 1962); *Man's Rage for Chaos* (New York: Schocken Books, 1965); and the one previously referred to, *Explanation and Power* (1979). Other philosophical sources providing partial confirmation can be found in Bryan Magee's excellent account of Schopenhauer's philosophy (on which this model is ultimately based), *The Philosophy of Schopenhauer* (Oxford: Clarendon press, 1983) and Malcolm Budd's recent book *Music and the Emotions* (London: Routledge and Kegan Paul, 1985). Budd's book was really the catalyst which stimulated me to devise this model. Other helpful sources are Edward A. Lippman, *A Humanistic Philosophy of Music* (New York: New York University Press, 1977); Victor Zucker-kandl, *Man the Musician* (Princeton: Princeton University Press, 1973) and Daniel A. Putman, "Music and the Metaphor of Touch," *Journal of Aesthetics and Art Criticism*, Vol. XLIV, No. 1, Fall 1985, pp.59-66. Support for this model from *linguistics* comes from Dwight Bolinger's recent work on intonation, which summarizes a lifetime of research in this topic, *Intonation and Its Parts: Melody in Spoken English* (London: Edward Arnold, 1986). There are many interesting observations in this fascinating book but the one of greatest relevance to our model of musical meaning is found on p. 74: "Power, as the manifestation of feeling, is the motive force behind intonation." This seems to link the will (power) with emotion (feeling) and "musical" pitch shapes (intonation). See also p. 221.

10. Roger Scruton, *The Aesthetic Understanding,* pp.85-86. There may be another dimension we should add, that of pain or pleasure. Malcolm Budd has devised a helpful model of an emotion, defining an emotion as a thought experienced with pleasure or pain" (*Music and the Emotions,* p.14). It may be that while the will's response is articulated in a wide variety of configurations of energy (as I have suggested), those configurations may be assigned a generally positive value (pleasure) or a generally negative value (pain).

11. Peter Rohner, "Will," *Encyclopedia of Theology,* ed. Karl Rahner (New York: The Seabury Press, 1975), p.1814.

12. Macolm Budd, *Music and the Emotions,* p.xii.

13. See George Sherman Dickinson, *A Handbook of Style in Music* (New York: Da Capo Press, 1969) pp.3-4, 106.

14. Victor Zuckerandl, *Man the Musician,* pp.31-43, especially page 39; Donald Ivey, *Song: Anatomy, Imagery and Styles* (New York: The Free Press, 1970) p.101; Morse Peckham, *Beyond the Tragic Vision,* expounding on Schopenhauer, pp.147-148.

15. Don Saliers, "The Integrity of Sung Prayer," *Worship,* July 1981, pp.290-303. The quotation is from p. 294.

3

The Mission
of the Church and Music

The main assertion I want to begin with is simple: As far as a theology of church music is concerned, the nature of *church music* is determined by the nature of the *church*, and the nature of the church is determined by its *mission*. This relationship between church and mission was well expressed by Adrian Hastings:

> It is, therefore, somewhat misleading to say that the Church has a mission, as if the existence of the Church comes first. In truth it is because of the mission that there is a Church; the Church is the servant and expression of that mission. The mission consequently dictates the nature of the church and insofar as the Church fails to live up to the demands of mission, it is effectively failing to be Church.[1]

Since the mission dictates the nature of the church and by implication the nature of church music, it is clear that we will need to consider the nature of the church's mission. I suggest that this can best be done under three headings: (A) the *basis* of the church's mission as the Trinity; (B) the *object* of the church's mission as the world; (C) the *purpose* of the church's mission as forgiveness. Each of these carries implications for a theology of church music.

A. The Basis of the Church's Mission

Since the primary meaning of the word *mission* is "send-ing," one must inevitably find the basis for the church's mission in the Trinity. This is explicitly stated in John 20:21-22 "Again, Jesus said, 'Peace be with you! As the Father has sent me, I am sending you.' And with that he breathed on them and said, 'Receive the Holy Spirit. If you forgive any-one his sins, they are forgiven; if you do not forgive them, they are not forgiven.' " Here the church is placed (under the apostles) right in the middle of the divine sendings or mis-sions; being sent by Christ with the same authorization as He was sent by His Father, and empowered by the same Holy Spirit which Christ received at his baptism (John 1:32-33), and which has now been poured out on the church (Acts 2:33). The mission of the church thus derives its basis direct-ly from the outgoing and self-sacrificing love of God the Father, Son, and Spirit. Any basis for the church's mission outside of this divine mission obscures the meaning of mis-sion and makes it unrecognizable for the world.[2]

It is from this source that church music also derives its mission. It too must learn to see itself as contributing to the great redemptive plans of God in its own way. Any other basis for church music is suspect and will ultimately fail. Church music is governed by the same constraints and moti-vated by the same redemptive concerns as God exhibits towards this world He has created, preserved, and redeemed. This leads to the next aspect under which we can view the church's mission—its object.

B. The Object of the Church's Mission

If God is the subject of the church's mission, what is its object? The Bible says that the object of the divine mission is the world. It is for this reason that the risen Lord com-mands his disciples: "Make disciples of all nations" (Matt.

28:19). This is why John described God as so loving the world "that he gave his one and only Son" (John 3:16). It is the world which is the object of the church's mission, as A. C. Krass has pointed out; "God's plan for the world is not that the Church will be saved. God's plan is rather to use the Church for the salvation of the world."[3] But what is this world like, to which the church, like Christ, is sent?

The world is not something which exists "out there" away from the church—the world is rather "the very form of man's being. . . . Men do not endure the world as something distinct from themselves. . . . they themselves 'are' the world."[4] It is within this world that Christians are called to live as citizens of two aeons, giving to Caesar what is Caesar's, "and to God what is God's" (Matt. 22:21). Yet also, as has been pointed out, it is a culturally diverse world in which the church must fulfill its mission. This cultural diversity also exists by the will of God, although it may never be absolutized and thus idolized by mankind. Its preservational and hence implicit redemptive function must never be obscured or forgotten.

These few observations carry great weight for church music. The music of church music can never be anything other than the music of human beings—creatures and sinners. There can be no division between being creaturely and being sinful.[5] Any attempt to create a music which is somehow closer to God or more sacred is thus as ridiculous as attempts to rid oneself of the taint of music regarded as somehow debased. All such efforts overlook the fact that we live in a fallen world, a world which we ourselves constitute as fallen. All Christian music making is done in this context. While pointing beyond this world, Christian music making is very much a part of this world. This means that the music of the church must be based on realistic considerations. As Thielicke has said, the Christian must know that "in principle he never gets in this aeon beyond the stage of compromise."[6] For church music this entails patience, understanding, courage, and, above all, love.

C. The Purpose of the Divine Mission

According to the New Testament, the heart of the gospel is the message about God's forgiveness offered to mankind in Christ. The thought of forgiveness is basic to the New Testament, even though it might not actually be expressed in those terms.

Forgiveness can be defined as "the action of God in the face of the sinful behavior of man, and is based on Christ."[7] The forgiveness offered by God through Christ means not only the eradication of guilt, "but also the restoration of fellowship, the retrieval of creatures by their Creator as acceptance into the life of God's eschatological reign".[8] Forgiveness therefore implies the following: There is a disruption in the relationship between God and mankind. God has moved definitively in Christ to restore that breach. Humanity was responsible before God's forgiveness was given and we are now responsible after hearing about His forgiveness. The forgiveness for sins offered by God in Christ is total and unrepeatable, encompassing the past, present, and future (Heb. 9:14; Rev. 13:8). This forgiveness cannot be earned or merited in any way, by any kind of behavior, otherwise it ceases to be forgiveness and mankind remains alienated from God (i.e. a person's sins are retained and God's judgment remains on that person, John 3:18).

For the one who accepts this forgiveness, it means that what Helmut Thielicke has described as "the aeonic nexus of guilt" has lost its claim to dominion over me (Rom 6:14): "That is, I am now characterized and determined, not by being 'in Adam,' but by being 'in Christ.' "[9] The Christian life then becomes from beginning to end a matter of being what one is, the juxtaposition of the indicative and the imperative. Another way of expressing it is to say that the

Christian must live every moment of his or her life in the conscious awareness of God's forgiveness: "It is only insofar, and so long, as I exist under forgiveness and take my orientation from it, that I can know the royal freedom of the children of God which is repeatedly promised me."[10]

The divine forgiveness of God, through which human beings can learn again to use freedom responsibly, is only available through Jesus Christ, according to the New Testament: "Salvation is found in no one else, for there is no other name under heaven given to men by which we must be saved" (Acts 4:12; 1 Tim. 2:5-6). In spite of the centrality of Christ in the purposes of God, the amazing and sobering fact is that Christ has committed this ministry of mediating forgiveness to the church. This is particularly clear in John's Gospel. Here the analogical identity between the Father's sending of the Son and the Son's sending of the disciples in the power of the Holy Spirit, has forgiveness as its end result: "If you forgive anyone his sins, they are forgiven; if you do not forgive them, they are not forgiven" (John 20:-23).

This is a task committed to the whole church. It represents the purpose of the church's mission—to mediate by act and word the forgiveness of God in Christ. It may not forgive on its own initiative without reference to the forgiveness of Christ which is the basis of this "fellowship of forgiveness."[11] But both aspects of the commission are important and both must be practiced by the church (forgiving and retaining) in fear and trembling, otherwise "forgiveness would be in danger of being trivialized."[12] To the extent that the church lives by and under the implications of forgiveness, to that extent the church is fulfilling its mission, a mission which has its basis directly in the forgiving love of God. What are the implications of this for Christian music making?

The acceptance of the fact that Christian existence is

based on and permeated with God's forgiveness in Christ through the Holy Spirit strikes simultaneous deathblows to attitudes which can be described as *musical legalism* and *musical lawlessness*. Musical legalism can be defined as the attempt to gain the approval of God by striving for musical perfection, or attempting to coerce others into doing the same thing for the same reasons (that is, gaining God's approval). The gospel message committed to the church states quite unequivocally that in Christ we already have the full and unconditional approval of God. There is nothing any human being is capable of which can alter that irrevocable acceptance available to mankind in Christ. Musical legalism attempts to undercut this and self-righteously imagines that aesthetic perfection is the only thing worthy of God. There is nothing that mankind has, is, or will do, which will make him any worthier or more acceptable in the sight of God than he or she already is in Christ. Christian music making, inside or outside the church, must be saturated in forgiveness. Forgiveness assimilated imparts a supple resilience, energized by love. Musical legalists, by contrast, believe in whipping themselves to greater and greater "aesthetic maturity," hoping that somehow this will impress God into being more gracious than He already has been in Christ.

The other side of the coin can be described as musical lawlessness. This would be the reverse of musical legalism and is an attitude which believes that God's unconditional forgiveness provides an excuse for irresponsible and slovenly music making, either inside or outside the church. Again, this attitude betrays a grave misunderstanding of what God's forgiveness is intended to result in. God's forgiveness does not mean an escape from responsible living but is a call back to responsible living motivated by a new self-concept defined by Christ and steadily formed as the individual cooperates with the Holy Spirit. A Christian musician who practices and advocates musical lawlessness is a person who wears his musical mediocrity every bit as self-righteously as the musical legalist wears his aesthetic perfectionism. Like the wicked and lazy servant of Christ's parable in Matthew 25:14-30, this person's lack of courage and faith in developing musical abilities to their full potential attempts to mask a basic hostility and hatred for God. ("I knew that you are a hard man. . . . So I was afraid" vv. 24-25).

The Christian musician is responsible to God for everything God has entrusted him or her with. Correctly discerning God's forgiveness in Christ liberates one to develop musically as far as one can in a spirit of freedom, joy, and discipline, the very antithesis of slovenly and irresponsible musicianship.

D. Conclusion

These are some of the implications one can draw for church music from the basis, object, and purpose of the church's mission. Although they have not been elaborated on at length, they are central to a theology of church music. Once they are lost sight of, the rest of the superstructure which is about to be built will collapse easily and disintegrate. They are therefore fundamental and foundational.

What is the superstructure which we can build on the foundations just laid? If we continue with the thought of the mission of the church, we are inevitably brought to the question (after specifying basis, object, and purpose) of the *means* of the church's mission. As we attempt to specify the means of the church's mission, we can discern a model of the church on which an entire superstructure begins to emerge within which we can develop a model of church music.

Notes

1. Adrian Hastings, "Mission," *Encyclopedia of Theology,* ed. Karl Rahner (New York: The Seabury Press, 1975) p.968.

2. G. C. Berkouwer, *The Church* (Grand Rapids: Wm. B. Eerdmans, 1976) p.398.

3. A. C. Krass, *Go. . . . and Make Disciples: Applied Theology I* (London: S.P.C.K., 1974).

4. Helmut Thielicke, *Theological Ethics: Foundations* (Grand Rapids: Wm. B. Eerdmans, 1976) p.436.

5. Thielicke, p.435.

6. Thielicke, p.487.

7. H. Vörlander, "Forgiveness," *New International Dictionary of New Testament Theology,* Vol 1, ed. C. Brown (Grand Rapids: Zondervan Publishing Co., 1975) 701-703. Quotation is from p.701.

8. Leonhard Goppelt, *Theology of the New Testament,* Vol. 1, (Grand Rapids: Wm. B. Eerdmans, 1981) p.131.

9. Thielicke, *Theological Ethics* p. 597.

10. Thielicke, p. 605.

11. Hans Küng, *The Church* (London: Search Press, 1968) p.331,

12. Vörlander, p. 703.

4

A Model of the Church

Basic to our model is the idea that the church, humanly speaking, is constituted by communication. This is not only verbal communication but also includes nonverbal communication. However, verbal communication is primary, while nonverbal is secondary. The church as a community exists through the spoken and written word. It is a network of people who sustain that network through language. The linguist M. A. K. Halliday has drawn attention to the similarities in this respect between schools and churches:

> Most other institutions. . . . serve their clientele in nonlinguistic ways. The hospital treats their ailments, the airline moves them from place to place, the hotel feeds and entertains them. In a school, the relation between staff and pupil is essentially one of talk. The whole function of the school is to be a communication network. . . . Perhaps the nearest type of institution to it in this respect is a church.[1]

Adapting Halliday's insight for our use, we may say that the relationship between Christians, which we call "church," is humanly speaking essentially one of talk. What is so fascinating about this is that if we look at the very first picture of the early church given us by Luke in the Book of Acts, it is a picture of a community whose very existence depends on talk. I am referring to Acts 2:42 which reads as follows; "They devoted themselves to the apostles' teaching and to the fellowship, to the breaking of bread and to prayer." The only activity which was nonverbal was the breaking of bread which would have been meaningless without a verbal commentary. It was through this communication network that the church existed as church. This was the *means* by which the church fulfilled its mission and it is still the same today. R. C. H. Lenski asserted that "the church has always felt that this [description in Acts 2:42] is a model,"[2] while Leonhard Goppelt asserts that what "this sentence enumerates are the basic elements of the Church's life."[3]

A closer look at this text which we can use as the basis for our model of the church and church music reveals the existence of *three distinct address-situations.* By this I mean three different types of communication had to occur for the church to fulfill its mission.

The first address-situation was that of the apostles proclaiming the message about Christ. This is a mode of communication where one person or a few people address the many. It is a monologue situation, one-way communication where the person making the address speaks to the people as if God were speaking to them. In 1 Thessalonians, Paul gave an accurate description of this mode of communication when he wrote:

> And we also thank God continually because, when you received the word of God, which you heard from us, you accepted it not as the word of men, but as it actually is, the word of God, which is at work in you who believe (2:13).

For Paul to have communicated with the Thessalonians in the beginning, he would have had to have spoken Greek. So the Thessalonians in fact *did* hear the message in human words. But in those human words they heard the words of God, repented of their sin, and accepted salvation in Jesus Christ. That is an excellent description of this mode of communication. Using the Greek word for the message of the gospel, we can call it the *kerygmatic* mode of communication.

The second type of address-situation we can discover in Acts 2:42 is hinted at by the words "fellowship" and "breaking of bread." Those who had responded to the kerygma about Jesus preached by Peter on the Day of Pentecost formed a new community in which sex, language, culture, creed, and color were transcended. The word for this new community is *koinonia*, fellowship. When the first Christians "activated" Christian fellowship, they were engaging in a mode of communication (both verbal and nonverbal) in which every believer was equal to every other believer. Unlike the kerygmatic mode in which there was a "hierarchy" in the communication process, in this mode everyone's communication was of equal value. They talked to each other and in so doing affirmed their mutual oneness in Christ. We could call this mode of communication *koinoniac*.

The third type of address situation in this verse is alluded to by the word "prayers." This is a different type of communication situation and is characterized by the many (the believers) speaking to the One (God). In this mode God is addressed directly as "You." We could call it the *leitourgic* mode of communication. A refinement which we must bring to the leitourgic mode is that it is a situation in which we address God not only in prayer, but also in praise. Here I made use of the ideas of Theodore Jennings when he described the Christian life as the alternation between prayer and praise.[4] (We will discuss this in more detail later.)

We are now at the stage where we can see how the full model looks. We will make use of a very helpful approach to understanding communication situations as presented by the linguist M. A. K. Halliday. The term "register" in linguistics signifies that the language we speak or write varies according to the situation. For us to describe any situation adequately, there are three elements: the nature and content of the activity (the field); the role relationships of those taking part in the activity (the tenor); and what function language is being used for in the activity (the mode). These three elements are present in any communication situation and enable us to understand what is happening in a precise way. What it does is to specify the context of the situation with precision. If we now apply this to the three modes of address the church uses to fulfill its mission, we get the chart known as figure 6. We now need to specify in greater detail what the kerygmatic, koinoniac, and leitourgic modes mean.

A. The Kerygmatic Mode of the Church's Existence

Perhaps the best place to start is with Gerhard Friedrich's comments on the proclamation of the gospel as described in the New Testament. He points out that the Greek word for preaching "does not mean the delivery of a learned and edifying or hortatory discourse in well-chosen words and a pleasant voice. It is the declaration of an event. Its true sense is 'to proclaim.' "[5] To the church has been committed this task of proclamation, this message about "Jesus Christ and him crucified" (1 Cor. 2:2). Yet the proclamation of the church is "more than historical instruction concerning the words and acts of Jesus."[6] It also proclaims the *significance* of that event, which consists in the fact that complete forgiveness is now offered by God in Christ for those who will repent and be baptized in the name of Jesus. This reception of God's forgiveness through Jesus is linked to the promise of the gift of the Holy Spirit (Acts 2:38; John 20:22-23).

One thing about the kerygma is certain: It did not originate with the church, but with God (1 Cor. 14:36). Paul often reminded the churches he founded of this fact, with these words: "What do you have that you did not receive?" (1 Cor 4:7). As J. C. Hoekendijk has said,

The apostolic preaching, the kerygma, was strictly objective.

	FIELD	TENOR	MODE
	1) Nature of the activity 2) Its content	Role relationships expected of participants	1) How the meanings are exchanged 2) What language is being used for
KERYGMATIC ADDRESS SITUATION	Proclaiming the forgiveness of God	Expected that the one speaking will speak with boldness and all will listen; relationship of disparity in the address – situation	1) Monologue – from speaker to audience 2) To confront
KOINONIAC ADDRESS SITUATION	Affirming the forgiven community	Expected that all may speak affirming the group and all will listen; relationship of parity in the address – situation	1) Dialogue – from speaker to speaker 2) To comfort
LEITOURGIC ADDRESS SITUATION	Prayer: Asking God for help	Expected that all will speak out of need and God will hear; relationship of disparity in the address – situation	1) Monologue – from audience to God 2) To request (express need)
	Praise: Thanking God for help	Expected that all will speak out of joy and that God will hear; relationship of disparity in the address – situation	1) Monologue – from audience to God 2) To thank

FIGURE 6:
THE THREE TYPES OF ADDRESS – SITUATION BY WHICH THE CHURCH FULFILLS ITS MISSION

> For this great history of God's acts there was apparently no
> point of contact in our life. We cannot use our own experi-
> ences to interpret or clarify what God has done.[7]

God's antipathy to human plans of salvation is clearly stated
in Ephesians 2:8-9: "It is by grace you have been saved,
through faith—and this not from yourselves, it is the gift of
God—not by works, so that no one can boast." This rejection by God of any basis for the gospel outside of His own
initiative extends even further, however. God does not only
intend a gospel which is foolish according to the wisdom of
this age (1 Cor. 1:20-21). Even the agents who proclaim that
gospel are described as foolish, weak, and lowly (1 vv.26-
28). All of this was done for one reason, said Paul, "so that
no one may boast before him" (v.29). If we believe that the
gospel originates with us, subject to our disposal, then we
have prostituted the gospel and emptied the kerygma of any
distinctively Christian content. It is now truly "a different
gospel—which is really no gospel at all" (Gal. 1:6-7).

If this is what the kerygma of the church involves, what
is the kerygmatic mode of the church? It is simply that
function of the church through which it declares or proclaims the gospel. The ways in which the kerygmatic mode
functions are many and varied, in both form and motivation.
The only thing that matters is that it is done. As to forms
of the kerygmatic mode, Paul's example remains determina-
tive for the church: he became a slave to the Jews, to those
under the law; to those not having the law, and to the weak;
"so that by all possible means I might save some" (1 Cor.
9:19-22). To guard against the misunderstanding that this
incredible variety in kerygmatic approaches might suggest
unbridled subjectivism on his part, Paul added that he did
all this "for the sake of the gospel" (v.23). As far as motiva-
tions for engaging in kerygmatic ministry, Paul was similarly indifferent. He accepted that some would proclaim Christ

out of envy, rivalry, goodwill, love, selfish ambition, and insincerity, concluding: "But what does it matter? The important thing is that in every way, whether from false motives or true, Christ is preached" (Phil. 1:15-18). This is not a matter for grudging acknowledgement, said Paul, but a matter for joy: "And because of this I rejoice" (v.18*b*).

As an illustration of some of the more common kerygmatic forms, Karl Barth's list of the ministries of the church is useful. The following activities he lists can easily be subsumed under the kerygmatic mode: preaching, teaching, evangelism, mission, theology, and prophetic action.[8] All of these activities involve proclaiming the gospel, an address situation which is exemplified in the Old Testament prophetic formula: "This is what the Sovereign Lord says" (Isa. 7:7; 10:24; 28:16; 30:15; Ezek. 5:5,7-8; Jer. 7:20; Amos 5:3). It is not only proclamation by word but also be deed. As Karl Barth has pointed out, one can say the same thing in another way, the speech of acts, made with hands as well as lips.[9] This observation must also be remembered in the other two modes, since the same applies: one communicates by actions as well as words. This model of the church is essentially a communication-based or semiotic model, not merely a verbal model.

The kerygmatic mode could be described as the declarative or proclamative mode which communicates God's acts and words of forgiveness for the world in Christ. It comes out of the blue, as it were, cutting across our expectations and values, and confronting us with a righteous and loving God. This gospel, the content of the kerygmatic mode, must be proclaimed, not only to those who have never heard it, but also to those who have heard it and need to hear it again: "The message does not lose it significance. Yet it must be proclaimed again and again, not just to the world, but to the community."[10]

B. The Koinoniac Mode of the Church's Existence

To define this mode one must first ask what fellowship means in the New Testament? F. Hauck found three basic meanings: to share with someone, to give someone a share in something, and in an absolute sense, fellowship.[11] It is clear that the underlying idea is one of relationship, either establishing, maintaining, or enhancing a relationship between persons. In Acts 2:42 (discussed earlier) the fellowship referred to by Luke denotes "the unanimity and unity brought about by the Spirit. The individual was completely upheld by the community."[12] The notion of fellowship comes to its fullest expression in Paul's writings, according to J. Schattenmann, and may not be understood as "the elimination of fusion of personality, but a new relationship based on the forgiveness of sins."[13] All of those who participate in this new relationship with God in Christ by the Spirit are not only differently related to God but are also differently related to each other. They form a new entity, a new fellowship unlike any other on earth. It involves new relationships and new responsibilities. A life forgiven entails a forgiving life within a community which is forgiven: "Be kind and compassionate to one another, forgiving each other, just as in Christ God forgave you" (Eph. 4:32).

The koinoniac mode (as an extension of these principles) would then involve the affirmation in, to, and within the community (though not stopping there) of God's forgiveness in Christ. It works out in community relationships the foregiveness which Christ by the Holy Spirit has worked and continues to work in the individual believer. It consists of words and actions embodying forgiveness in the address situations of the believer to him or herself, and of believer(s) to fellow believer(s) in the community.

What is important in the koinoniac mode is the absence of hierarchical considerations and the emphasis on equality and reciprocity. In Romans 1:11-12, Paul seems to show a transition (almost in the actual moment of composing his sentences) from the necessary hierarchical role implied by his apostolic (read: kerygmatic) function to his place in the koinoniac mode of the church, where he is "just another believer," giving and receiving in equality: "I long to see you so that I may import to you some spiritual gift to make you strong—that is, that you and I may be mutually encouraged by each other's faith."

While the koinoniac mode is characterized by equality and reciprocity in terms of participation, its aims are always positive and constructive. To make more explicit what types of activities are customarily koinoniac in nature, the following list (by no means comprehensive) is taken from Barth's discussion of the church's ministries: cure of souls, personal examples of Christian living, diaconate, and fellowship.[14]

C. The Leitourgic Mode of the Church's Existence

Through the repentant and baptised response of people to the kerygma, the koinonia is formed by the Spirit under the head, Christ, "created in Christ Jesus to do good works" (Eph. 2:10). The believing response to the kerygma, on which basis the koinonia is formed, is now taken up into the most comprehensive mode of the church, the *leitourgic* mode. All the issues which have emerged from the kerygmatic and koinoniac address situations come to a climax and culminate in the leitourgic address situation. All of this is magnificently expressed in articles 9 and 10 of the Constitution on the Sacred Liturgy:

9. The sacred liturgy does not exhaust the entire activity of the Church. Before men can come to the liturgy they must first be called to faith and to conversion. . . .

10. Nevertheless the liturgy is the summit toward which the activity of the Church is directed; at the same time it is

the fountain from which all her power flows. For the goal of apostolic works is that all who are made sons of God by faith and baptism should come together to praise God in the midst of his church, to take part in her sacrifice, and to eat the Lord's supper.[15]

In this excerpt the operation of and distinction between the various modes is clearly seen. The kerygmatic mode is distinguished by phrases like "called to faith" and "conversion" and "apostolic works." A phrase like "come together" refers to the koinoniac mode. The leitourgic mode is indicated by the phrase "praise God." What is also significant in this excerpt is that the liturgy is the summit toward which all the church's activities are directed. Unlike the kerygmatic and koinoniac functions which often occur independently of each other in time and space, the leitourgic mode is integrative. In essence, its function is to pull together all the various threads of the other modes into one address-situation in which God is addressed by people in the alternation of prayer and praise. It is usually the most routinized of the modes, its actions occurring at regular times in regular places, involving the coordination of the greatest number of people at one time. More than any other mode, the leitourgic mode is where the public face of the church as church is shown to the world and to itself. In its operation it includes kerygmatic and koinoniac modes of address, while subsuming (without denying their independence) these modes within the highest level of Christian existence—that of worship. It is fundamentally in the worship of the congregation, wrote Hans Küng, where "the Church is, where the Church, the community, happens."[16]

In seeing the leitourgic mode as a successive alternation of prayer and praise, use is made here of Theodore Jenning's valuable discussion of this topic. Jennings's most helpful insight is in the way he distinguished between prayer and praise, a difference which he called "both deceptively simple and deeply significant."[17] On the one hand, prayer "expresses our need and desire for God, a need that grows out of our godlessness and godforsakenness." Praise, on the other hand, is the expression of "our joy in and gratitude for God's presence."[18] These, according to Jennings. are "the two fundamental actions of our common worship: together in alternation they give worship its structure and rhythm. . . . prayer and praise are distinguished by the absence and the presence of God."[19]

We could say, keeping to the emphasis on forgiveness, that the leitourgic mode is an alternative between the expression of our need for God's forgiveness (prayer) and our response to the fact that in the forgiveness offered in Christ we have all that we need (praise). We have now discussed the three modes by which the church fulfills its mission in some detail.

Three tasks remain in this chapter: to show how the three modes are interrelated and interdependent, to show what theological support there is for this model of the church and to show how the three address-situations have their counterparts in the Bible.

D. The Relationships Between the Three Modes

In general, the three modes are to be thought of as interconnected and interdependent modalities. All three are needed for the church to fulfill its mission of mediating the message and fact of forgiveness to an alienated world. No mode can be eliminated without affecting the other modes. In specific terms, as has been pointed out the kerygma is strictly objective and derives from no other source or initiative than God and God alone. The kerygmatic mode is therefore by definition the foundation of the other two modes. As Paul put it, "no one can lay any foundation other than the one already laid, which is Jesus Christ" (1 Cor. 3:11).

The koinoniac mode, it is clear from the New Testament, depends totally for its operation on the proper functioning of the kerygmatic mode. The biblical position can be stated quite bluntly: no kerygma, no koinonia. The basis for churchly koinonia (and there is no other, according to the New Testament) is the koinonia of the believer with Christ. That koinonia only comes about through repentance, baptism in His name, the reception of the forgiveness of sins, and the gift of the Holy Spirit (Acts 2:38). The warning of J. C. Hoekendijk with regard to koinonia is highly relevant here: "We must not speak too quickly of community. Only insofar as men are partakers of the shalom, represented in the kerygam, do they live in mutual communication and fellowship."[20]

Problems in the koinoniac mode arise when it loses its moorings in the kerygma. The community is only and always constituted by virtue of the gracious acts of God in Christ: "It is because of him [God] that you are in Christ Jesus" (1 Cor. 1:30). If it loses touch with this basis, it has no option but to depend more and more on its own resources whether those be cultural, political, aesthetic, or social. Hans Urs von Balthasar has described such a community as one which, perhaps subconsciously, celebrates itself more than it celebrates God.[21]

The same sort of interdependence as exists between the kerygmatic and koinoniac modes pertains to the relationship between the koinoniac and leitourgic modes. The sequential dependence of the modes is therefore as follows: no kerygma—no koinonia—no leitourgia. This relationship is well expressed in the remarks by D. H. Tripp that "alienation from worship is alienation from that community. Most fundamental is alienation from the faith on which the community is built."[22] An important corollary of the interdependence of the three modes is that changes in one mode will of necessity cause changes in other modes. An example of this is liturgical reform which proceeds in defiance of problems accumulated in the kerygmatic and koinoniac modes. Reforms in the leitourgic mode made without reference to problems in the other modes are likely to be no more than cosmetic and may even serve to deepen frustration. Joseph Gelineau illustrated this when he questioned whether many of the people in a given service have the kind of human relationships between each other which enable them "to hear the word in common in a fruitful manner, really to share their prayers, and brotherly communion." He concluded on the basis of Acts 2:42: "It is probably no accident that Acts put koinonia before the prayers and the breaking of bread."[23]

As far as the interrelationship of the three modes is concerned, then, they are interconnected and interdependent, with the leitourgic mode depending upon the koinoniac mode which in turn depends upon the kerygmatic mode. This is illustrated in figure 7.

E. What Support Is There for This Model Of the Church?

In contemporary theology there has been a tendency to develop models of the church using categories denoted by key theological terms from the Greek New Testament. To facilitate evaluation and comparison of these models, a sample of nine have been chosen and they are tabulated side by side in the diagram which follows (see fig. 8).

On examining this diagram it is obvious that neither the concept of the church as martyria (witness), nor the concept of the church as institution have commanded widespread acceptance. This does not mean that either are unimportant but only that, in terms of a sample of current discussion, these ideas of the church remain somewhat marginal. There is fairly solid support for kerygma as a category describing a function of the church (seven out of nine), koinonia (nine

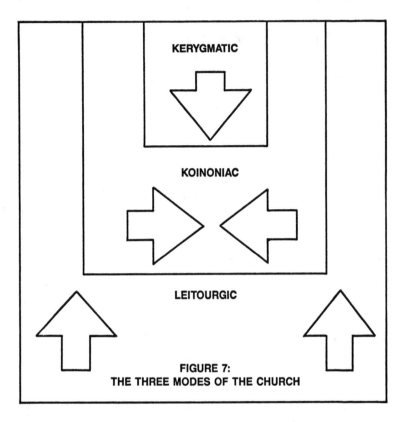

FIGURE 7:
THE THREE MODES OF THE CHURCH

out of nine), diakonia (eight out of nine) and leitourgia (six out of nine). The model proposed in this study (kerygma, koinonia, and leitourgia) is closest to Gelineau's model.[33] Apart from diakonia as a category or function it is evident from this diagram that there is substantial support for a kerygmatic-koinoniac-leitourgic model of the church. Diakonia cannot be included, in my opinion, because the linguistic evidence suggests that this term covers the whole of Christian existence, not just one aspect of it.[34]

As distinguished a theologian as Dietrich Bonhoeffer used Acts 2:42 (the source for the kerygmatic-koinoniac-leitour-

HOEKENDIJK[24] (1966)	DULLES[25] (1974)	KELSEY[26] (1975)	TRIMP[27] (1978) (DUTCH)	GELINEAU[28] (1978)	NXUMALO[29] (1979)	BOSCH[30] (1980)	MOODY[31] (1981)	DESCHNER[32] (1982)
						MARTYRIA (an inclusive concept for the 4 below)	MARTYRIA	
KERYGMA	HERALD	KERYGMA	HOMILETIEK EVANGELISTIEK CATECHETIEK	TEACHING	EVANGELIZATION	KERYGMA		
KOINONIA	MYSTICAL COMMUNION	KOINONIA	POIMENIEK	KOINONIA	KOINONIA	KOINONIA	KOINONIA	FELLOWSHIP
DIAKONIA	SERVANT	DIAKONIA	DIAKONIEK		DIAKONIA	DIAKONIA	DIAKONIA	SERVICE
	SACRAMENT		LITURGIEK	PRAYERS	WORSHIP	LEITOURGIA		WORSHIP
	INSTITUTION							

FIGURE 8:
CONTEMPORARY MODELS OF THE CHURCH IN CHRONOLOGICAL ORDER

gic model) as the basis for the ecclesiology he developed in
The Cost of Discipleship. His words as to the importance of its
first phrase in particular are unequivocal: "Every word in
this sentence is significant."[35] After stressing the importance
of the Word of God as the word spoken through human
words,[36] he pointed out that the fellowship is mentioned
between the reference to the Word (the apostles' teaching)
and to the Sacrament (the breaking of bread and prayers):
"This is no accident, for fellowship always springs from the
Word and finds its goal and completion in the Lord's Supper.
The whole common life of the Christian fellowship oscil-
lates between Word and Sacrament."[37] It is interesting to see
that Bonhoeffer saw the three means by which the body of
Christ is made visible as Word-Fellowship-Sacrament.[38]
These are identical with the kerygmatic, koinoniac, and lei-
tourgic functions as I have discussed them.

F.   The Three Modes in Relation to the Bible

To develop as comprehensive a basis for church music as
possible, it is necessary to specify the relationship between
the proposed model and Scripture. What is referred to here
is not the matter of the scriptural basis for the model of the
church discussed, since its scriptural basis has already been
established. Rather, it is the discovery that there exists an
important relationship between the kerygmatic, koinoniac,
and leitourgic modes of the church and certain modes of
address within Scripture which modern hermeneutics appears to have uncovered. Before this relationship can be
precisely stated, however, certain biblical data must be no-
ticed.

In the words of Hans Küng, "It is the word which creates
the Church and constantly gathers it together again by
arousing faith and obedience."[39] This importance of the
word in the early church is clear from an examination of its
occurrences in the New Testament. It is not only the sayings

of Jesus which are important and which will never pass away (Matt. 7:24-26; 24:35; Mark 13:31; Luke 21:33). After the resurrection and ascension of Jesus and the Day of Pentecost, a phrase which became more and more important is "the word of God" (Acts 4:31; 6:2,7; 8:14; 11:1; 12:24, 13:5,7,44; 17:13; 18:11; 19:20). This usage was sometimes broadened to "the word of the Lord" (Acts 8:25; 13:48-49; 15:35-36; 16:32; 19:10). Often, it was just abbreviated to "the word" (Acts 4:4; 6:4; 10:44; 11:19; 14:25; 16:6; 17:11). The early Christians were brought into a new relationship with God by that word (Jas. 1:18; 1 Pet. 1:23). That Word, explains Peter and Paul, is nothing other than the gospel itself (1 Pet 1:23-25); Col. 1:5). Supremely, of course, in John's Gospel, the Word is with God, is God, and was made flesh—here the identity between the Word which is the gospel and Christ is made unforgettably explicit (John 1:1,-14).

Response to this Word, which is Christ the good news of God, involves a nonverbal component. According to Peter, Christian wives can, by Christlike behavior, influence their non-Christian husbands to accept the Word without speaking a word (1 Pet. 3:1). James clearly delineated that both verbal and nonverbal aspects are inseparably part of response to that Word which is Christ: "But the man who looks intently into the perfect law that gives freedom, and continues to do this, not forgetting what he has heard, but doing it—he will be blessed in what he does" (Jas. 1:25). Specifying that the word of God cannot be reduced to merely human words, although it is unavoidably expressed that way, Paul wrote: "When you received the word of God, which you heard from us, you accepted it not as the word of men, but as it actually is, the word of God" (1 Thess. 2:13). In short, "the word of God" was defined in the New Testament comprises the following features: (a) Although expressed in human words, it is not identical with those words; (b) the response to that expression involves both hearing and doing together as equal and complementary activities; (c) the content of the Word is none other than Christ Himself, His sayings and actions, especially in John's Gospel; d) the word of God has its corporate aspect in the growth of the church. For Luke, the growth of the word of God is seen in the growth of the church (Acts 6:7; 12:24; 19:20).

In greater detail, this process entails the following aspects. At an early stage, this "word of God" ("the word of Christ and the word about Christ")[40] became codified by the church in a fixed yet flexible tradition (1 Cor 11:2; 2 Thess. 2:15; 3:6) or teaching (Acts 2:42; Rom. 6:17; Titus 1:9). Its means of transmission, also at an early stage of the community's history, were twofold: oral transmission and written transmission (e.g., "Stand firm and hold to the teachings we passed on to you, whether by word of mouth or by letter," 2 Thess. 2:15; see also Col. 4:16; 1 Thess. 5:27; 2 Pet. 3:15-16).

The cumulative effect of this church-generated process of transmission was that the word of and about Christ came to be codified in what we know today as the New Testament Scriptures. There is thus a reciprocal relationship between church and the New Testament canon of Scripture. The church's self-understanding is reflected in the documents it produced, a self-understanding which in turn it maintains by continued reference to those documents. At a more abstract level this is to say that a doctrine of the church co-entails a doctrine of Scripture. This is because the formation and continuation of the one (the church) goes hand in hand with the formation and the continuation of the other (the New Testament Scriptures). As Leander Keck has pointed out, "the Bible as canon cannot be separated from the church."[41] But the Bible's relation to the community is a dialectical one. On the one hand, the traditions that the

Bible contains "served as warrants for the community's life, on the other hand, those same traditions and texts became the criteria of its life. . . . the canon both legitimates and judges the community."[42]

While Keck's dialectic primarily refers to the New Testament canon, J. A. Sanders had observed the same phenomenon a few years earlier with the Old Testament canon. Sanders discerned two hermeneutic modes which are operative in the structuring of the biblical traditions, the constitutive and the prophetic: "The one tended to read the tradition in a constitutive or supportive way, while the other permitted the tradition to be read in a challenging way."[43] By grouping the synonyms of these two writers together, one can get a picture of the two aspects of this relationship between the community and the Scriptures: warrant, legitimates, constitutive, supportive/criterion, judges, prophetic, challenging.

Yet there is a third aspect to the relationship between community and Scripture which is still needed if one is to do justice to the full range of address-situations which the Bible as a whole intends to include us in. Both for the Old Testament and the New, biblical scholars have insisted that one of the most powerful formative contexts of the biblical writings is that of worship. The norm by which ancient Israel weighed the adequacy of theological statements, wrote Harvey Guthrie, was determined by what a community of faith "knew and experienced and was involved in as it proclaimed its identity in worship."[44] As far as the New Testament writings are concerned, Martin Hengel asserted that all of them, including the Gospels, "grew out of worship, the focal point of the earliest church, and were written to be used in worship (1 Thess. 5:27). They have come down to us only because they were read in worship."[45] So, in addition to confrontative and comforting uses of the Scriptures, the church has always used the Scriptures liturgically, even as they were being formed, collected, and edited. It is not only that the Scriptures can function very appropriately in address-situations of challenge, comfort, and worship. It is also that it is precisely these same types of address-situations in the life of the faith community which were decisive in the formation processes of the biblical writings. A correct use of the Bible will make use of these three modes in its reading of Scripture. Since they emerge directly out of the canon-forming process itself, a high degree of validity should inhere in such a hermeneutic, according to Sanders.[46]

As the church allows itself to be addressed by the Bible in these three address-situations, the truth of Küng's statement is clear: It is the Word which creates the church.

Obviously, from a human point of view, the reverse is also true: It is the church which creates the Scriptures, a fact evident from the foregoing discussions on the canon. What is significant is that, starting from independent starting points, the three functions of the church as discussed dovetail exactly with the three address-situations evident in Scripture. This is indicated in figure 9.

This way of conceptualizing the relationship between church and Scripture makes it clear that the task of the church and the various address-modes of the Scriptures coincide in bearing witness to the Word of God, Jesus Christ, as He is present in the prophetic/kerygmatic, constitutive/koinoniac, and liturgical/leitourgic modes of address. (The relevance of this insight for church music will be explored later.) What needs to be stressed here is that neither the church nor the Scriptures are the focus of attention—it is what they point to that matters. The word or message which is communicated by word and deed within and by means of these communicational structures is none other than Jesus Christ, the Word of God. It is the articulation of that Word in proclamation, affirmation, and worship which is the common thrust of church and Scripture. This Word of God is not

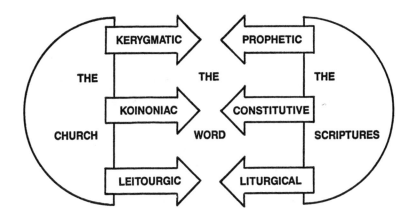

FIGURE 9:
THE THREE MODES OF ADDRESS
IN CHURCH AND SCRIPTURE

to be casually identified with either church or Scripture or both.

Here the comments of Otto Weber are particularly helpful. He began by insisting that biblical faith is not faith in the Bible, but faith in the God of the Bible: "We believe the Bible only when we believe *in* the Word of *God* which sounds through it."[47] Similarly, drawing on the Reformation view that Scripture authenticates itself only because God authenticates it through His Spirit, Weber asserted that "the church is not understood primarily as the divinely established teaching institution but rather as the place of proclamation."[48] Neither the Scriptures nor the church, therefore, have any authority apart from their witness-bearing function: "The Bible is authoritative only when, *in* the variety of voices the One Voice is heard. . . . Without the Word of God witnessed to it in Scripture. . . . the Church for its part would have absolutely no authority."[49]

Once again, there is a circular relationship between the

church and holy Scripture, as discussed: The Scriptures would not exist without the church, but, likewise, neither could the church continue to exist without continually returning to the Scriptures. Theologically speaking, the function of both is to bear witness in many words and different address-situations to the one Word of God, Jesus Christ. Two scriptural texts confirm this relationship (John 5:39-40; 1 John 1:1).

In the Johannine version of one of Jesus' confrontations with some Jewish people, Jesus says; "You diligently study the Scriptures because you think that by them you possess eternal life. These are the Scriptures that testify about me, yet you refuse to come to me to have life" (John 5:39-40). Similarly, in the Epistles of John, the role of the community of believers (the church) as no more and no less than bearing witness to the Word of God is made clear: "That which was from the beginning, which we have heard, which we have seen with our eyes, which we have looked at and our hands have touched—this we proclaim concerning the Word of Life" (1 John 1:1). So both texts affirm that the Scriptures point to Christ, the Word, and so does the community of believers.

The church's mission is therefore fulfilled as it allows the Bible to speak the word of Christ in prophetic, constitutive, and liturgical ways. The critical words are of course, "as it allows." There is nothing automatic in this process. Every day, every week, every year, every decade, in each historical epoch, culture, and geographical region, the church has to ensure that this happens. It so happens that this task is a theological task (that is, it has to express to each contemporary generation of human beings in ways they can hear so as to understand this message about Christ). The Bible's teachings must be assimilated, interrelated, systematized, interpreted according to the history of the church, and then applied to each new generation of believers. There is no magic inherent in the Bible whereby if we saturate the world with the Scriptures in their usual form, the world will come to salvation. We have to find out its meaning for us today. That is no easy task, as Paul implied when he wrote to Timothy; "Do your best to present yourself to God as one approved, a workman who does not need to be ashamed and who correctly handles the word of truth" (2 Tim. 2:15). Paul himself was not content with the mere restatement of texts from the Old Testament, and neither was Jesus. Both used Scripture interpretively, and applied it to new generations of believers (that is, they used the Bible theologically).[50]

These comments are directly relevant as we move to consider a model of church music based on the model of the church proposed earlier. This is because any model of church music has to deal with Colossians 3:16, the Magna Carta of church music, and its key phrase is "Let the word of Christ dwell in you richly." That word is a message about Christ which is found nowhere else *except* in the Bible, but it is not identical with the Bible itself. In other words, church musicians are also called, whether they like it or not, to "correctly handle the word of truth" as Paul wrote. (See 2 Tim. 2:15). Again, that is a theological task involving assessing the meaning of ancient biblical documents for our lives, our times, our today, so that the word of Christ may dwell richly in our hearts. With that, let us now turn to an analysis of Colossians 3:16.

Notes

1. M. A. K. Halliday, *Language as Social Semiotic* (London: Edward Arnold, 1978) p.232.

2. R. C. H. Lenski, *The Interpretation of the Acts of the Apostles* (Minneapolis: Augsburg Publishing House, 1934) p.117.

3. Leonhard Goppelt, *Apostolic and Post-Apostolic Times* (London: A and C. Black, 1970) p.42.

4. Theodore Jennings, *Life as Worship* (Grand Rapids: Wm. B. Eerdmans, 1982) pp.126-139.

5. Gerhard Friedrich, *Theological Dictionary of the New Testament*, Vol III, ed. G. Kittel (Grand Rapids: Wm. B. Eerdmans, 1965) p.703.

6. Friedrich, *TDNT*, Vol III, p.711.

7. J. C. Hoekendijk, *The Church Inside Out* (London: SCM Press, 1966) p.25.

8. Karl Barth, *Church Dogmatics*, Vol IV, Part 3, Second Half (Edinburgh: T and T. Clark, 1962) pp. 867, 870, 872, 874, 879, 895.

9. Barth, p.862.

10. Friedrich, *TDNT*, Vol III, p.711.

11. F. Hauck, *Theological Dictionary of the New Testament*, Vol III, ed. G. Kittel (Grand Rapids: Wm. B. Eerdmans, 1965) pp.804, 808.

12. J. Schatteman, "Fellowship", *New International Dictionary of New Testament Theology*, Vol. 1, ed. C. Brown (Grand Rapids: Zondervan Publishing Company, 1975) p.642.

13. J. Schattenman, *NIDNTT*, Vol 1.

14. Barth, *Church Dogmatics*, pp.885, 887, 889, 898.

15. Walter M. Abbott, ed. *The Documents of Vatican II* (London: Geoffrey Chapman, 1967) p.142.

16. Hans Küng, *The Church* (London: Search Press, 1968) p.235.

17. Theodore Jennings, *Life as Worship* (Grand Rapids: Wm. B. Eerdmans, 1982) p.11.

18. Theodore Jennings, *Life as Worship*, 126.

19. *Ibid.*

20. J. C. Hoekendijk, *The Church Inside Out*, p.23.

21. Hans Urs von Balthasar, "The Grandeur of the Liturgy," *Communio*, Vol V, No 4, Winter, 1978, pp.344-351. The reference is from p. 347.

22. D.H. Tripp, "Worship and the Pastoral Office," *The Study of Liturgy*, ed. C. Jones, G. Wainwright and E. Yarnold (London: S.P.C.K., 1978) 510-532. The quotation is from p. 516.

23. Joseph Gelineau, *The Liturgy Today and Tomorrow* (London: Darton, Longman and Todd, 1978) p.51.

24. J. C. Hoekendijk, *The Church Inside Out*.

25. Avery Dulles, *Models of the Church* (Dublin: Gill and MacMillan, 1974), n.p.n.

26. David Kelsey, *The Uses of Scripture in Recent Theology* (London: SCM Press, 1975), n.p.n.

27. C. Trimp, *Inleiding in de Ambtelijke Vakken* (Kampen: Copieer-inrichting v.d. Berg, 1978), n.p.n.

28. Jospeh Gelineau, *The Liturgy Today and Tomorrow*, n.p.n.

29. J. Nxumalo, "Church as Mission," *Journal of Theology for Southern Africa*, Vol. 26, March 1979, pp.38-49.

30. David J. Bosch, *Witness to the World* (London: Marshall, Morgan and Scott, 1980), n.p.n.

31. Dale Moody, *The Word of Truth* (Grand Rapids: Wm. B. Eerdmans, 1981), n.p.n.

32. John Deschner, "What Does Practical Theology Study?" *Perkins Journal,* Vol xxxv, No 3, Summer, 1982, pp.8-16.

33. Joseph Gelineau, *The Liturgy Today and Tomorrow,* pp.49-52.

34. H.W. Beyer, *Theological Dictionary of the New Testament,* Vol III, ed. G. Kittel (Grand Rapids: Wm. B. Eerdmans, 1964), pp.81-92.

35. Dietrich Bonhoeffer, *The Cost of Discipleship* (London: SCM Press, 1959) p.224.

36. *Ibid.*

37. *Ibid.*

38. *Ibid.*

39. Küng, *The Church,* p.375.

40. Martin Hengel, "Hymns and Christology," *Between Jesus and Paul* (London: SCM Press, 1983) 78-96, see p. 80.

41. Leander Keck, "Toward a Theology of Rhetoric/Preaching," *Practical Theology,* ed. D. Browning (San Francisco: Harper and Row, 1983) p.132.

42. *Ibid.*

43. J. A. Sanders, "Hermeneutics," *Interpreter's Dictionary of the Bible,* Supp. Vol. ed. K. Crim (Nashville: Abingdon Press, 1976) p.405.

44. Harvey Guthrie, *Theology as Thanksgiving* (New York: Seabury Press, 1981) 182.

45. Martin Hengel, "Hymns and Christology," p.xiii.

46. J. A. Sanders, "Hermeneutics," p. 403.

47. Otto Weber, *Foundations of Dogmatics,* Vol I (Grand Rapids: Wm. B. Eerdmans, 1981) p.18, (author's emphasis).

48. *Ibid.* p. 249.

49. *Ibid.* pp. 20, 251, (author's emphasis).

50. There is ample justification for speaking of a theological use of the Bible. See the excellent work of David Kelsey in this area: *The Uses of Scripture in Recent Theology* (London: SCM Press, 1975) and "The Bible and Christian Theology," *Journal of the American Academy of Religion,* Vol. XLVII, No. 3, 1980, pp.385-402. See also Peter Stuhlmacher, *Historical Criticism and Theological Interpretation of Scripture* (Philadelphia: Fortress Press, 1977) pp.22-24.

5

A Model of Church Music

I. The Theological Foundation: Colossians 3:16

The most explicit scriptural statements about church music are contained in Colossians 3:16 and its parallel passage in Ephesians 5:18-20: "Let the word of Christ dwell in you richly as you teach and admonish one another with all wisdom, and as you sing psalms, hymns and spiritual songs with gratitude in your hearts to God" (Col. 3:16). The great German writer on the theology of music, Oskar Söhngen, recognized the centrality of this text for church music and began his treatise *Theologie der Musik* (1967) with an exposition of Colossians 3:16. Any model of church music must do the same. For this reason, the results of more recent exegesis on this text will be covered in an attempt to lay the theological component of a model of church music. As far as the relationship between this text and Ephesians 5:18-20 is concerned, Martin Hengel recently concluded that "the text of Ephesians is dependent on that of Colossians and is the first commentary on it."[1] For this reason we will concentrate on Colossians 3:16.

The first phrase of this text is "Let the *word of Christ* dwell in you richly" (author's italics). Hengel found it striking that this formula is used only here in the New Testament. In his opinion, "the author wants it to emphasize the christological determination of the word proclaimed in worship."[2] More simply, Peter O'Brien took it to mean "the message that centers on Christ."[3] It is this message that the Colossians were to allow to "live/dwell" or "be present" in their community.[4] The manner in which this process of "allowing" (an implicit appeal to their wills) is to occur is significant: "richly." Hengel translated this as "abundance," noting that it also has the meaning of "in a constantly new way."[5]

The next part of this text is: "as you teach and admonish one another with all wisdom, and as you sing psalms, hymns and spiritual songs." The punctuation of this passage is problematical, since neither the commas nor the "and" supplied by the *New International Version* and the Revised Standard Version are in the original Greek text. The most satisfying solution is the one recently proposed by O'Brien. His preference is for joining "psalms, hymns and spiritual songs" with "teaching and admonishing one another." O'Brien cited four reasons favoring the elimination of the comma after "wisdom": (i) the symmetry of the two participal clauses "in all wisdom teaching. . . ." and "with grace singing. . . ."; (ii) the insertion of an "and" which is not in the original Greek test; (iii) the parallel passage in Ephesians 5:19 gives the same interpretation if O'Brien's solution is adopted; (iv) early Christian hymns had both didactic and hortatory elements and so could be used to teach and admonish.[6] Hengel also favored this interpretation, suggesting that the punctuation of the Nestle text in Colossians 3:16 is incorrect. Basing his conclusions on Clement of Alexandria, Westcott and Hort, Lightfoot, Lohmeyer, and the understanding of this text by the author of the Letter to the Ephesians, he wrote that "the psalms, hymns and spiritual songs" is presumably to be connected with the preceding participles *teaching* and *admonishing*.[7] This teaching and admonition in all wisdom "arise from the indwelling of the word" and it is, as O'Brien remarked, the members who teach and admonish one another.[8]

Distinctions between the terms *psalms, hymns,* and *spiritual songs* are also problematical from the point of view of the exegesis of this text. The basic problem is not that there is no intrinsic reason for distinguishing between them. Even exegetes like Bartels and Hengel end up suggesting some degree of difference between the terms.[9] The nub of the problem was stated by G. Delling when he asserted that it is scarcely possible to distinguish the three terms absolutely from each other "because of the small number of passages in the New Testament for comparison."[10] We should therefore be cautious about going to either extreme with these terms: They are possibly distinctive forms in relation to each other but just how distinctive, we have no way of knowing at the present time. In the words of E. Lohse, these three terms taken together "describe the full range of singing which the Spirit prompts."[11] Since the adjective "spiritual" applies to all three,[12] and these songs are "gifts of the Spirit"[13] we are to understand the categories as spiritual psalms, spiritual hymns, and spiritual songs.

The final phrase of Colossians 3:16 is "sing. . . . with gratitude in your hearts to God." O'Brien interpreted this phrase to mean "the attitude or disposition which is to accompany the previously mentioned instruction and admonition."[14] Commenting on the phrase "sing . . . in your hearts to God," Hengel maintained that this phrase designates "the liturgical song . . . produced in the heart to the praise of God."[15]

Taken as a whole, O'Brien has provided a fitting summary of Colossians 3:16 as the theological basis for a model of church music: "As the word of Christ indwells the members of the community and controls them so they teach and admonish one another in Spirit-inspired psalms, hymns and songs."[16] Echoing these sentiments, H. Schlier remarked that "the spiritual song of the Church is the Word of Christ uttered in the cultus in the form of alternating and reciprocal address."[17] But notice that there are two address-situations: to "one another, . . . to God." Since both the kerygmatic mode and the koinoniac mode are "to one another," all three address-situations can occur in the use of music in the church: to one another—kerygmatic; to one another—koinoniac; to God—leitourgic.

From this point of view, Colossians 3:16 can be seen as the musical version of Acts 2:42. For the church to fulfill its mission, it will have to make use of three distinctive types of church music: kerygmatic music, koinoniac music, and leitourgic music.

We are now in a position to outline a model of church music. First of all there is a diagram of the model (figure 11). Second, I will provide a detailed discussion of each category, column by column.

II.   A Model of Church Music

This model of church music connects the three modes by which the church fulfills its mission: kerygmatic, koinoniac, and leitourgic, with the theology of church music evident in Colossians 3:16: communicating with one another and with God through song. But it also attempts to integrate many aspects of the preceding pages to provide a comprehensive model of church music. Since it is very condensed in its present form, I will go through each column and explain it in detail (see fig. 11).

The basic idea is that there are three types of church music: kerygmatic music, koinoniac music, and leitourgic music, and that each is especially adapted to the function it must serve in the life of the church. This model is an application to music of a key concept in linguistics—the difference between a *dialect* and a *register*.

The distinction between a dialect and a register arose because linguists were trying to find a meaningful way to account for varieties in language. A dialect accounts for language which varies according to the *user* whereas a register accounts for variations which occur due to *use*. The difference between British English and American English, for example, is a variation due to dialect. The difference between the language an American college student would use in addressing his roommate in the dormitory as compared with addressing the college president is a variation due to register.

It is extremely helpful to apply the same concept to account for variations in music. For example, your favorite style of music is likely to be the one that was most part of your life in your adolescence.[18] No matter how many years have passed, that music is your type of music, your musical dialect, if you will. Yet all of us deal with music which varies according to use, not only according to user. Music which is being used to tranquilize us as we deal with the stress of spending money in a supermarket is very different from the use of music in a live concert. In the latter the performer's job is to grab our attention with his/her music, and the music is the reason for the event. I have adapted Halliday's chart on dialect and register, and applied it to music in figure 10.

Musical Dialect	*Musical Register*
— musical variation according to the user.	— musical variation according to the use.
A musical dialect is: - what you sing, play or listen to habitually - determined by who you are (socioregion of origin and/or adoption) - expresses diversity of social structure	A musical register is: - what you are singing, playing or listening to at the time. - determined by what you are doing. - expresses diversity of social process
So, in principle, musical dialects are:	So, in principle, musical registers are:

- different styles communicating similar meanings (as in a love song in pop music, soul music, or country music)	- ways of saying different things (as in worship music as compared with evangelistic music as compared with funeral music as compared with wedding music).
- differences in styles but the meaning of the songs are the same.	- music is being used to mean different things.
Principal controlling variables in a musical dialect:	Principal controlling variables in a musical register:
- Social class	- field (type of social action)
- geographical origins	tenor (role relationships)
- generation	mode (use of music in this situation)
- age	
- sex	
Characterized by:	Characterized by:
- strongly held attitudes towards musical dialects (read: styles) as a symbol of social diversity.	- a sensitivity to musical registers as symbols of diversity in social processes.

Figure 10: Musical Dialects and Musical Registers[19]

The model of church music I am proposing here deals with musical registers rather than musical dialects. In other words, the variety of styles (read: musical dialects) one could use in church is theoretically infinite. In practice, it would tend to be defined by variables such as social class, geographical region, generation, age, and sex. Yet the major problem as I see it in church music is to separate the issue of musical styles (dialects) from the issue of what we are trying to use music for in a given situation. We need to differentiate between musical variations due to different *users* of music and musical variations due to different *uses* of music. Generally, a style would remain the same across many different uses, but not across many different users. Country music as a style could be used as Muzak, at a live concert, or as worship music in a church. It could not be used with people who did not know, understand, or like country music.

This has the important outcome that this model of church music can be used with any group of users because it deals with differences in the uses of music. It would work just as well in a church in Sri Lanka as in Sacramento, because it deals with uses of music in the church rather than users of music.

A. Kerygmatic Music

1. Field: *What is to be communicated and what is being done*

The content of kerygmatic music is obviously the kerygma. We have discussed this in some detail in the section on the kerygmatic mode of the church. Everything said there about the content of the kerygma applies to the content of kerygmatic music. Its content is to bear witness to the salvation we find from God because He has completely and unconditionally forgiven us through the death of Christ. There are many aspects to the gospel and we should not expect every song to spell out every aspect in minute detail. Kerygmatic songs have an "objective" quality to their texts (that is, they are frequently studded with factual statements; as in "Christ the Lord is risen today."). Frequently kerygmatic texts are in the third person singular (as in, "He is Lord.") When a more personal kerygmatic statement is needed, as in songs of witness or testimony, first and second person pronouns abound (as in, "I know whom I have believed.")

Whatever the exact grammaticaly realization, kerygmatic songs aim to do one thing: proclaim the gospel. They are didactic in the best sense of the word: they aim to pass on a message. An interesting feature about kerygmatic music is that frequently the addressee—the person to whom the text is addressed—is oneself (that is, one can and should proclaim the gospel to oneself in song, as well as to others). "Tell Me the Old, Old Story" is a beautiful example of a

MUSICAL REGISTER / ADDRESS SITUATION

FIGURE II: A MODEL OF CHURCH MUSIC	1. FIELD		2. TENOR (Relationship between participants)			3. MODE	
	What is to be communicated	What is being done	Degree of formality	Intragroup relations	Disposition of the will	How the meanings are exchanged	What the song's function is in this situation
KERYGMATIC MUSIC	Communicate the forgiveness of God	Proclamation	Formal	Soloist or specialized group relating to a generally non-specialized group	Boldness	Mono-directional: From performer to audience (One singing; all listening)	To confront people—focus is on the message
KOINONIAC MUSIC	Communicate that it is good to belong to the fellowship of those forgiven	Affirmation	Informal	Semi-specialized or non-specialized group relating to semi-specialized or non-specialized group within the context of the larger group	Unity and togetherness	Omnidirectional: Reciprocity and equality of exchange emphasized (All singing; all listening)	To comfort people—focus is on the needs of the community
LEITOURGIC MUSIC	Communicate a need for God	Supplication	Formal	Non-specialized group (The congregation) relating to God in the directness of leitourgic address	Desolation	Mono-directional: The congregation sings to God, who is the audience (Kierkegaard) (All singing; God listening)	To plead with God—focus is on the absence of God
	Communicate the presence of God	Thanksgiving	Formal	—	Jubilation	—	To praise God—focus is on the presence of God

MUSICAL REGISTER / ADDRESS SITUATION

FIGURE II: A MODEL OF CHURCH MUSIC	4. GENERAL ORIENTATION OF THE MUSIC STYLE	5. LEVEL OF MUSICAL REPLICABILITY	6. RELATIONSHIP TO CULTURAL DIVERSITY	7. RELATIONSHIP TO THE ADDRESS-SITUATIONS OF SCRIPTURE	8. RELATIONSHIP TO RITUALS OF CHURCH AND COMMUNITY
KERYGMATIC MUSIC	Since the emphasis is on the message, styles can change radically and thus tend to be innovative in profile	Low level of musical replicability: compositions tend to be the preserve of the specialized originating group	Fairly high tolerance in this mode for culturally diverse musical styles	Tends to use declarative, pro-clamative and prophetic themes from the Scriptures	Can be used in any ritual context where kerygmatic elements are to be stressed.
KOINONIAC MUSIC	In koinoniac music, styles tend to be midway between highly innovative (kerygmatic), and conservative (leitourgic)	Medium level of musical replicability: compositions tend to be quite "learnable" by the group as a whole	Medium tolerance in this mode for culturally diverse musical styles, pro-vided there is no conflict with the need for group consensus	Tends to use supportive, comforting and constitutive Scriptures for context	Can be used in any ritual context where koinoniac elements are to be stressed.
LEITOURGIC MUSIC	Once styles for leitourgic music are established they tend to change slowly and also to resist any further change	High level of musical replicability: compositions have stabilized over longer periods than kerygmatic and koinoniac music—they are generally familiar to a much larger group of people than the other two modes	Low tolerance for culturally diverse musical styles, since this is where a group is at its most vulnerable point before God	Tends to use Scrip-tures which articulate the absence of God ___ Tends to use Scrip-tures which articulate the presence of God	Can be used in any ritual context where leitourgic elements (prayer and/or praise) are to be stressed.

kerygmatic hymn in which the singer, in asking someone to tell the old, old story is actually speaking to herself as well as to us: "Tell me the story often, For I forget so soon, The early dew of morning has passed away at noon."

2. Tenor: *Degree of formality, intragroup relations, and appropriate dispositions of the will*

Kerygmatic music is generally performed in a formal setting, because it is monodirectional (that is, one-way communication). In a kerygmatic setting (this will also be discussed under "Mode"), it is expected that someone will deliver a "message" and the rest of the group will listen. There is no provision made for communication from the audience, in the same mode as the performer presents it, other than alternative means (as in, clapping, walking out, sleeping, yawning, laughing, and so forth). It is in this sense that kerygmatic music is performed in a formal setting.

The intragroup relations in the kerygmatic setting usually involve a soloist or a specialized musical group addressing a nonspecialized group. For one reason or another, the role occupied by those communicating the message is specialized. For example, a person may have an average voice compared with the level of musical ability, in the congregation. Yet when he or she stands up to sing "Amazing Grace," for example, the singer occupies a specialized role for the duration of the song. Usually, however, only people who can handle the role of being a musical specialist will be asked to occupy the role. The kerygmatic situation is a listening situation and it is expected that what one is listening to is, at least, as good as the congregational level and, in most cases, a good deal higher in ability level.

In terms of types of musical events, the soloist and/or specialized musical group (a choir) seems to be the one best suited to carry out the task of kerygmatic music. Choirs, for example, are meant to be listened to, even if they are behind the congregation, which is already an indication that they are meant to function in a kerygmatic address-situation. Vague talk about the choir "leading" worship only obscures the vital differences between kerygmatic music and leitourgic music. Only the congregation as a whole unit can engage in worship, in leitourgic music. The choir can indeed lead worship but they must do so in a manner and from a position which makes their connection with the congregation clear (as when the choir stands among the congregation). It is unbiblical to imagine for one moment that the choir can worship God "on behalf of" the congregation. Rather, the choir is at its best when it addresses the congregation kerygmatically.

In leitourgic music the choir joins the congregation as an indivisible part of that congregation in its prayerful and praiseful address of God. Strictly speaking, the choir as choir cannot function well in koinoniac music either. The reason for this is that koinoniac music (as well as seen shortly) is marked by complete equality, reciprocity, and mutuality in its function. It is difficult to achieve this equality through involving the choir as choir because of the associations it rightly carries with the kerygmatic address-situation, a situation in which all expect musical specialization and musical innovation above the average ability level of the congregation. Only in pieces where the levels of musical complexity are comfortably within the reach of both congregation and choir can the choir retain its separate role in koinoniac music. Otherwise, it destroys the equality of the koinoniac address-situation which is its essence.

Nicholas Temperley's comment on the aesthetics of the church's hymns is relevant here, when he wrote that "the criteria for acceptability are not the same for a participant as for a listener. . . . hymns exist for the singers, not for an audience, still less for a critic."[20] Kerygmatic music, unlike koinoniac and leitourgic music ("hymns" in Temperley's statement), exists for the benefit of an audience of listeners. The other two types are designed for address-situations which signify active, equivocal participation and, therefore, as Temperley has indicated, the aesthetic criteria of acceptability are different. (We will discuss this further under the heading "Level of Musical Replicability").

How does one act in a kerygmatic address-situation? The Bible is quite clear on this point—boldness characterizes the proclamation of the gospel. As P. Davies has written, " 'Boldness' in the New Testament becomes almost a stock term to describe the standing, the manner, and the spirit of those who proclaim the gospel."[21]

This boldness is not a confidence in oneself—it is derived from the new experience of boldness before God which Christ has made possible. Openness and boldness toward men in proclaiming the gospel come from a new relationship with God. This ties in with the model of musical meaning discussed earlier, where it was suggested that music is meaningful to us because its shapes suggest affinities to the shape of our wills in a particular situation. Kerygmatic music must proclaim the gospel boldly, openly, sincerely, and frankly. The specific musical realization of this boldness will vary from song to song, person to person, situation to situation, and culture to culture. But that boldness has to be there if kerygmatic music is to be authentic. Any musical setting of the gospel message that smacks of timidity and fearfulness, seeming to apologize for itself and afraid of disapproval from those who are not believers, or even those who are believers, is itself not true to the gospel.

3. Mode: *How the meanings are exchanged and what the song's function is*

We need to look more closely at how the meanings are exchanged in a kerygmatic address-situation. A helpful way to do this is to use Nattiez's model of the musical event, as in figure 12.

This structuring of the musical event reflects a "soloistic" orientation, with the interpreters "passively" listening to a group-dominating performance.[22] This event involves a communication by one person or a few people to relatively many people. The standard "concert" format for a musical event is an illustration of a kerygmatic address-situation. Notice that it is monodirectional (that is, the participants in the address-situation expect that the flow of communication will be one-way—from the producer to the interpreter through the music).

This helps to clarify what the song's function in a kerygmatic address-situation. Its role is to confront, to startle, to challenge, to provoke a response. Kerygmatic music concentrates much more on the message being communicated than the other modes of church music.

4. General Orientation of the Musical Style

Since kerygmatic music is only concerned with getting a message across, it tends to be the least rigid of the three modes of church music. It can and must be as innovative as possible within the constraints of whatever context it finds itself. Whatever style of music communicates the gospel boldly and clearly according to convergences of person, group, culture, and historical moment is acceptable kerygmatic music, "so that by all possible means I might save

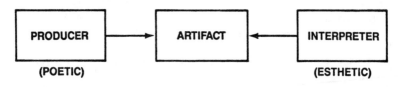

FIGURE 12:
A "KERYGMATIC" ORIENTATION TO THE FUNCTIONAL TRIPARTITION

some" wrote Paul (1 Cor. 9:22). Kerygmatic music needs to grab the attention of disinterested listeners and confront them with its message.

It is speculative and open to debate but there is the possibility that certain styles of music may be more suited to one or other of the modes of church music. For example, a musical style that is highly aggressive (loud, fast, and heavily accented), operates in a formalized concern setting, is characterized by a high degree of innovation within its genre, suggests the likelihood that such a style is more suited to kerygmatic purposes than other styles. By these criteria, rock music would be more suited as kerygmatic music than, say, folk music. Admittedly these are broad generalizations, since much of Bob Dylan's pre- and post-conversion music is highly kergymatic (using kerygmatic in a more generalized sense, only here, of "prophetic"). Still it is interesting that Dylan switched from his folk idiom a few years ago and used more electrified instrumentation and the idioms of rock music. Perhaps within the context of developing Western culture, Dylan realized that rock music was now more appropriate as a kerygmatic vehicle than folk music at that time.

5. Level of Musical Replicability

This important concept is based on the assumption that all human beings have a greater or lesser musical ability. There is probably no human being who does not have some ability, however limited, to respond to music. In people designated by society and/or themselves as musical, this ability is explicit and cultivated to a lesser or greater degree (that is, they are defined or they define themselves, as "musicians" of one sort or another). In people designated by society and/or themselves as "nonmusical," this ability is implicit and not cultivated, although, strictly speaking, the adjective "nonmusical" is incorrect since it is extremely unlikely that there could be any such category as "a completely nonmusical human being" (that is, a human being with absolutely no capacity whatever to respond to any kind of human music making, past or present). Everyone, therefore, has some musical ability, explicit and highly developed in some individuals, ranging across the spectrum to those whose musical ability is latent and underdeveloped.

In the second place, to respond to music in any way, at any level, a person needs a certain amount of knowledge. According to Otto Laske, this knowledge is partly *declarative* (knowledge of musical structures) and partly *procedural* (knowledge which ensures that the individual has the capacity at a given level of engaging in music-making activity). He illustrated the difference between the two types of knowledge as follows: "To know what is a major scale is declarative knowledge, but to play a major scale on the piano presupposes procedural knowledge."[23] Using this very useful distinction between declarative and procedural musical knowledge, we can see that the precise "mix" of declarative and procedural musical knowledge in any given individual will be a function of his/her life history within a given culture or cultures. The concept of levels of musical replicability as it appears in the diagram of a model of church music is a concept indentical with what Laske defined as procedural musical knowledge. More precisely, Laske defined procedural musical knowledge as "a practical, experiential knowledge concerning the procedures required for producing, analyzing, and understanding music."[24]

The differences between the two kinds of musical knowledge (declarative and procedural) are important for our model of church music because it enables us to specify the level of musical replicability appropriate to each of the three types of address-situation. For example, kerygmatic music involves an address-situation of a few communicating to the many. As such, it makes specific demands on the *declarative* musical knowledge of the audience while making demands on the *procedural* musical knowledge of the performers. A member of an audience preparing to hear Handel's *Messiah*, for instance, could reasonably be expected to have a minimal declarative musical knowledge of this work (perhaps its form, historical background, and style), even though that person may have a low procedural knowledge of this work (that is, be unable to sing or play the music of the *Messiah* to a level acceptable to a given reference group). Conversely, whatever the declarative musical knowledge of a performer in Handel's *Messiah*, his or her procedural knowledge must be higher than that of the majority of their audience. A performance situation is no longer credible when the performers are less capable than the average ability-level of their audience. The usual response in a situation like this is for the audience to redefine the situation as a nonperformance situation at that point. That is, they walk out or engage in other kinds of behavior which attempt to undermine the performance-situation by calling the performer's status in question (as in booing or hissing). As far as the level of musical replicability required in a performer-oriented musical event is concerned, it is low as far as the audience's procedural musical knowledge is concerned (that is, they do not have to be able to sing or play the music to ensure that this particular address-situation succeeds).

The consequences of this are that music for kerygmatic address-situations tends to belong to the specialized group producing it. For example, there are very few pieces composed by contemporary Christian music groups which have become the common property of the singing congregation. The reason for this is self-evident: Musically, the demands of a kerygmatic address-situation call for music which will grab the listener's attention. It is therefore more complex and accompanied by sophisticated instrumentation and recording techniques. Andrae Crouch is one of the few sophisticated contemporary Christian musicians whose songs have become congregational songs. But even then, when one considers his total creative output, the number of his songs that have managed the crossover is limited to two or three (for example, "To God Be the Glory"). The crossover effect with inspirational music (for example, the Gaithers) is much greater for the simple reason that much inspirational music is not actually kerygmatic music in the sense defined here. It is better understood as koinoniac or leitourgic music. Its corresponding level of musical replicability is much higher than for kerygmatic music (i.e., it is much easier to sing).

6. The Relationship of Kerygmatic Music to Cultural Diversity

What is relevant here is also relevant to koinoniac and leitourgic music. It is evident that there are specific differences between the operation of the kerygmatic mode on the one hand and the koinoniac and leitourgic modes on the other hand. Whereas in the kerygmatic mode one presents the gospel in whatever cultural forms are appropriate at the time of proclaiming it (as Paul did), in the koinoniac and leitourgic modes one is inevitably involved in a certain degree of cultural adaptation. In the kerygmatic mode one's commitment to cultural forms is on a short-term and pragmatic basis. In the koinoniac and leitourgic modes the commitment to cultural forms of a specific kind is on a long-term basis.

While one may justly indicate the divine origins of the church by such phrases as "the church as the people of God," or "the church as the creation of the Spirit," or "the church as the body of Christ,"[25] the church is very clearly a human community. Like all human communities, the church has its own inbuilt tendency to perpetuate itself. If this self-perpetuation is done without reference to Christ, the head of the church (Eph. 4:15), it is no longer a Christian koinonia and it is incapable of authentic leitourgia. Yet in spite of this, the koinonia has to make discreet allowances for this tendency of human communities (of which the church is one) to perpetuate themselves.

The emphasis here is on the phrase "discreet allowances," because in the first instance the koinonia must insist upon its prior and foundational unity in Christ, which transcends yet is not separable in this age from whatever lesser unities may be contributed by various sociocultural factors native to the community in question. These allowances must be made, not only because cultural diversity exists as a preservational structure by God's providence, but because the very nature of the koinoniac mode requires the affirmation, however relative and conditional, of the human (cultural) factors which are germane to those in that community. Ethelbert Stauffer has asserted that while economic, social, sexual, national, and historical differences are transcended in the church, they are not removed.[26] As pointed out, the coming of Christ has meant the relativization of these preservational structures but not yet their elimination. This dialectic is expressed in Stauffer's conclusion that "early Christianity knows only one saving event, the cross, and only one Church. But this is neither a national church nor a universal Church; it is the Church of the nations."[27]

There is an excellent illustration of this in Acts 6:1-7. Hengel insisted that we take the problem of language seriously in this incident, saying that the differences in the languages spoken by the community "would necessarily and quickly have led to separate worship, since at least a considerable number of the "Hellenists" could only have followed Aramaic worship partially, if at all."[28] Making reference to the criterion of edification, Hengel maintained that in the long run " 'edification' in a service held in a foreign language would not have come up to the standard which Paul at a later date regarded as a sine qua non in Corinth for a proper service."[29] In effect, the early community in Jerusalem divided into two groups,[30] based on language differences, which, of course, inevitably involved cultural differences.

This striking occurrence, given the high degree of unity which was a characteristic of the early church, must be seen, as Stauffer has noted, as the emergence of the church of the nations. The result is that while in the kerygmatic mode the approach to culture is utilitarian, pragmatic, and functional, the koinoniac and letourgic modes require the church to take culture a lot more seriously. Yet the church cannot afford to ever take culture to seriously in view of the fact that Christ has stripped all preservational structures of their power over human beings (Col. 2:15, 17, 20-23).

7. The Relationship of Kerygmatic Music to the Address-Situations of Scripture

As discussed in the section on the three modes of the church in relation to Scripture, the Bible both in its history of formation and in its completed canonical form presupposes three types of address-situation: the prophetic, the constitutive, and the liturgical. What we find in kerygmatic music is that it tends to make use of declarative, proclamative, and prophetic themes from the Scriptures. For example, the kerygmatic song, "Have you any room for Jesus?" is quite clearly based on the Gospel writer's observation that "there was no room for them in the inn" (Luke 2:7). Luke wanted to contrast the true nature of Jesus with the reception He received in our world as a kerygmatic (that is, confrontative element). The hymnwriter picked up on this theme and fashioned a kerygmatic song. Naturally there are thousands of such themes in the Bible, providing an incredibly rich resource for the maker of Christian songs.

8. The Relationship of Kerygmatic Music to the Rituals of Church and Community

Again, much of what is said here will be applied to koinoniac and leitourgic music, but in less detail.

The model of the musical event as developed by Nattiez is helpful in understanding how the process of musical meaning operates. Yet the musical event is most often embedded in other events in which extramusical considerations play an overriding part. What I am referring to here is that the musical event usually occurs in a ritual context of some sort. Research done by anthropologists and ethnomusicologists shows that there is a universal association of music and ritual in all human cultures.[31] This is not difficult to understand if one remembers that music offers human beings a way to affirm their identities (as constituted by their wills) and that ritual is concerned with "movement across social boundaries from one social status to another" and that it acts as "the interval marker in the progression of social time".[32] While ritual signifies transition, music signifies the consolidation and maintenance of the persona. Since ritual is a necessity in such transitions, music also becomes essential.

Rituals occur both inside and outside the church and we use them to mark transitions or movement through social space (as in from being unmarried to being married) and through social time (as from December 31, an "ordinary" day, to January 1 New Year's Day). This division corresponds roughly to the distinction anthropologists make between *calendrical* and *noncalendrical* rituals. Calendrical rituals are rituals tied to socioeconomic periods which are cyclical and recurrent, while noncalendrical rituals are occasional or crisis rituals (as in drought), and life-cycle rituals (as in birth, puberty, marriage, and death). Whatever the ritual, "all ritual is directed toward the problem of transformations of state in human beings or nature."[33]

The fact is that both inside and outside the church, ritual is a fact of life. The question is not whether we will have ritual inside and outside the church or not, but rather: what kinds of rituals shall we have and what will be their meanings? The church has its own distinctive rituals, and so does the surrounding culture. The members of a church are also members of a culture and have ritual obligations to both. The rituals of a church and its surrounding culture offer invaluable opportunities within which the church can fulfill its mission.

Because of the constant association of music and ritual, church music has a tremendous role to play in the life of the church and the community. For example, there are relatively few songs of theological and artistic merit in most churches for the important ritual transitions of baptism, the Lord's Supper, birth, puberty, marriage, and burial. The few songs there are for these transitions also fail to be anthropologically aware of the dynamics of a particular ritual, for example, Christian marriage. This is a transition which creates whole new networks of relationships for many people and this is seldom addressed in the ceremony or the music used.

There are also numerous other smaller transitions which are significant in the life of the church and could be marked with simple rituals and music especially developed for those rituals. This whole area is almost completely undeveloped in church music and offers fertile soil for much musical endeavor by the musicians of the church. As an aid to this, figure 13 attempts to show a few of the ritual possibilities for any church in any culture.

As far as kerygmatic music is concerned, there are kerygmatic elements in most situations and if it is desired to emphasize those, they can be with good effect. For example, a funeral is ostensibly a ritual for helping the living make the transition from having one of their number alive to adjusting to one of their number being dead. From a Christian perspective, a funeral is a tremendous opportunity to proclaim an aspect of the gospel (as that Christ has overcome

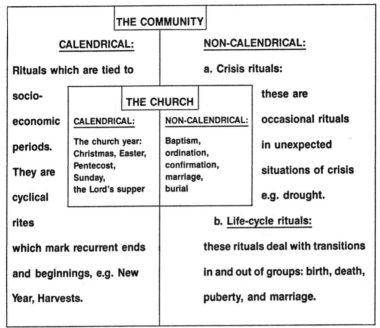

FIGURE 13: THE CHURCH IN A RITUAL CONTEXT

death). This can be effectively done through an appropriate song on this theme. In this way, the church can help relate the gospel to people in transition in a most powerful way. Many times it is only at points of crisis (signified most deeply in ritual) that an individual is prepared to consider God as a meaningful part of his or her life.

Naturally, this is an area where the church can easily betray its mission. If the church's rituals and calendars mesh exactly with those of its surrounding culture in such a way that its distinctive Christian message is indistinguishable from certain cultural imperatives, then the church has become the world and has lost its soul. If, on the other hand, the rituals and calenders of the church have no meaningful points of contact with the rituals and calendars of its sur-

rounding culture, then the church through self-absorption
has also betrayed its mission.

As far as church music is concerned, the same possibilities
and dangers which a ritual approach offers are offered to a
church music which has the courage to take a ritual approach seriously. As long as it is aware of the dangers and
seeks to minimize them, a ritual approach to church music
offers tremendous potential.

B. Koinoniac Music

1. Field: *What is to be communicated and what is being done*
Koinoniac church music, being the musical expression of
the koinoniac mode as the affirmation of fellow believers,
exists to articulate every aspect of our common life in Christ
as a common life characterized by a unity-in-diversity. It is
imbued with a spirit of unity, a finding of consensus among
people who differ, more or less widely. Koinoniac music can
only be produced and appreciated by those who know their
community and by those who really care about music which
edifies and affirms everyone in that community: the young
and the old, the poor and the rich, the wise and the simple,
the faithful and the faithless. Erik Routley has beautifully
expressed the spirit that animates true koinoniac music
making. He began by observing that many successful hymn
tunes have been written not by great composers but by
ordinary ministers of religion. The reason for this, he said is
that:

> they knew what it was like to stand in a pew and sing.
> . . . It is not only a question of writing less music than one
> would otherwise write, nor is it a matter of rebelliously ac-
> cepting the limitations of the unmusical community. It is a
> matter of liking the people who are going to sing the hymns,
> and that means "welcoming the duty" in a truly gospel
> sense.[34]

Perhaps the reason there is so little truly koinoniac music around today is that the musical writers and performers (for whatever reasons) do not really like "the people who are going to sing the hymns." It has become fashionable in some quarters to denigrate and berate the church for its addiction to artistic and musical mediocrity.[35] Ultimately, however, without love, even the most gifted music maker sounds worse than "a resounding gong or a clanging cymbal" (1 Cor 13:1). Recent archaeological research indicates that what Paul was referring to with the words "resounding gong" was really a series of thirteen tuned bronze vases arranged around the back of Greek amphitheaters which were used to amplify the actor's voices. William Harris concluded that Paul was saying that without love "I am as empty as the acoustic amplifiers of the Greek theatres, full of sound but literally saying nothing in the decadent years of Hellenic achievement."[36] "Love covers over a multitude of sins," Peter told us in 1 Peter 4:8, and presumably that coverage includes the "sin" of musical mediocrity. We must always remember that one person's mediocrity is another person's perfection.

Music which polarizes and alienates people is not koinoniac music. It may be kerygmatic music, which in its prophetic function becomes a stumblingblock and foolishness to those who are angered that anyone should have the temerity to meddle with their own "do-it-yourself" schemes of salvation (1 Cor. 1:23). In the case of kerygmatic music one may definitely and rightly have polarization and alienation. This is all part of the fact that the gospel brings judgment as well as grace, darkness as well as light (2 Cor. 2:14-16). But koinoniac music deals in edification, helps, affirmation, constructive growth after kerygmatic surgery. It is saturated with mutuality, reciprocity, and a spirit of actual and potential unity. It is comforting but not comatose, soothing but not tranquilizing. Carlton Young has well expressed the ethos of koinoniac music in these words: "This is hard to explain, but as an example, the gathered community may just want to express through song its sense of togetherness and it can be led to share in the feeling through song."[37]

2. Tenor: *Degree of formality, intragroup relations and appropriate dispositions of the will.*

Koinoniac music is characterized by informality. People are meant to be comfortable with koinoniac music because its function is to affirm and build up the community. There is no place here for formality and hierarchy. Koinoniac music signifies the community with its defenses down, relaxed, and happy.

An example of how the intragroup dynamics are handled in koinoniac music occurs when a performer will sing the verses of a song and invite the audience to sing the chorus of the song with him or her. In traditional church music the ancient practice of antiphonal and responsorial singing is a similar example, a practice which could easily be revived in the church today on a much wider scale.

The dispositions of the will we need to encourage musically in koinoniac music are those of unity and togetherness. The exact musical realization of this will vary from style to style and culture to culture but it will not be the jagged harsh melodic lines one might use to make a point in kerygmatic music. The melodic line will be more flowing, easy on the ear, and user-friendly.

3. Mode: *How the meanings are exchanged and what the song's function is in this situation*

We can modify Nattiez's diagram to show that it is involved in koinoniac music. In koinoniac music we try to bring the producer/performer of music much closer to the interpreter/listener/(see figure 14) than they would be in a kerygmatic address-situation.

This kind of address-situation can and does occur in musical events where the distinction of poles is still retained to a small degree, but there is far greater interchange, equivalency, and equitability between the two functions. In figure 14 the poetic (performer-producer) and esthetic (interpreter-audience) poles are still distinguishable, but in their realisation of the musical event, both sets of participants stand midway between a group-dominating event (as in figure 12) and a group-dominated event (see figure 15). This structuring of the address-situation could be described as one in which subgroups alternate and exchange roles in a climate of equality and mutuality. Koinoniac song is therefore omnidirectional (i.e. the stimulus for singing and the songs can come from any individual or any group within the group). No one is better or worse in koinoniac music making, everyone is accepted for who they are. Reciprocity and equality of contribution are emphasized, unlike kerygmatic music. Whereas kerygmatic music is vertical, in the sense that God (in the person of the singer) speaks to us from above, koinoniac song is strictly horizontal—all can sing and all can listen.

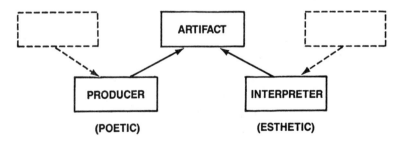

FIGURE 14:
A "KOINONIAC" ORIENTATION TO THE FUNCTIONAL TRIPARTITION

The function of koinoniac song is to focus on the needs of people in a caring and loving way. The community needs this kind of song otherwise it can build no settled sense of who it is and what it is like. It needs to feel comfortable with itself and that all who are there belong to it by an indissoluble bond. Koinoniac song is a wonderful way to accomplish this goal.

4. General Orientation of the Musical Style

Because of its emphasis on constructive building up of the community, koinoniac music cannot afford to be too radical in style but neither can it be too conservative. It has to match stylistically the music that people are comfortable with, both as listeners and as active participants in the singing. Any style that the community defines as middle of the road, relaxing, easy-listening music will be an acceptable style for koinoniac music.

Sometimes a performer will use a structured kerygmatic address-situation like a concert to do koinoniac music, music which is affirmative and group enhancing. In this category we would place performers who have an entertainment orientation. Frequently, they are maligned by the Christian public as having "sold out" to popularity, money, or whatever. Provided the performer is a professing and practicing believer, there can be no harm in this and indeed much good. It is the failure to distinguish between kerygmatic music and koinoniac music that causes problems here. When an audience defines kerygmatic music as the only type of Christian music which is valid, there will be no room for the koinoniac music maker. This is a real pity because, as will be stressed later on, all three types of church music are essential to the life of the church. An unbalanced approach emphasizes one type at the expense of the others.

5. Level of Musical Replicability

Koinoniac music, because of the function it has to fulfill in the mission of the church, will utilize styles which are not difficult for people to learn. They will not be as simple as the styles used in leitourgic music, nor will they be as complex as kerygmatic music.

Unlike kerygmatic music, which is more performer oriented, the more participator-oriented modes of church music, starting with koinoniac music and supremely in leitourgic music, place increasing demands on the procedural musical knowledge of a greater number of people, that is, the levels of musical replicability increase from medium to high. In koinoniac and leitourgic music the ideal is that everyone must be able to participate musically at an acceptable level. This can be a formidable challenge to church music today as there is very little true community singing in modern Western societies. Music in the koinoniac and leitourgic modes of address is simpler musically than kerygmatic music because these modes cannot function without the active involvement of everyone present. The larger the group required to sing, the greater the "spread" of musical abilities and consequently the lower the common musical denominator has to become. The ability to replicate satisfactorily a certain musical artifact is not important in a kerygmatic musical event, because the understanding in such a event is that one or few will address the musical communication to many, who will listen and not "perform." However, the ability for people to replicate musical pieces (to engage their procedural musical knowledge in a given instance) becomes more important as one moves to the koinoniac and leitourgic musical events. An inability to replicate a certain musical artifact in either the koinoniac or leitourgic modes will frustrate and hinder the smooth functioning of those address-situations, as when the organist chooses a tune for a well-known hymn text

which no one knows (that is, they are unable to replicate
that musical artifact in a procedural way).

6. The Relationship of Koinoniac Music to Cultural Diversity

To reiterate what was said earlier under kerygmatic music
and cultural diversity: in koinoniac music one has to make
a firmer commitment to cultural forms which matter to the
community than with kerygmatic music. Foreign musical
styles which were tolerable in the kerygmatic address-situation are not so bearable when we have to find music which
speaks of who we are and where we come from. It has to be
music from closer to home. Yet, there is still an openness to
a certain variety of styles in this area, particularly in urban
areas.

7. The Relationship of Koinoniac Music to the Address-Situations of Scripture

Because we are concerned with building up the community in koinoniac music, this type of address-situation will
favor Scriptures which comfort and affirm rather than question and condemn. It is not that we have lost sight of the
gospel in koinoniac music—it is just that there are people
who are hurting, who are lonely, who find it hard to trust
people and trust God. They need to be encouraged, inspired,
and motivated to go on. Positive scriptural themes like the
love of God and oneness in Christ are important in koinoniac music. Each mode of church music highlights aspects of
the Bible which are indispensable to the church. It is all part
of letting the Word of Christ dwell richly in our hearts
through music.

8. The Relationship of Koinoniac Music to Rituals of Church and Community

Koinoniac music functions better in a ritual context than
either kerygmatic or leitourgic for the simple reason that

ritual concerns community and changes in an individual's status with respect to his or her community. A koinoniac use of music can be incredibly valuable in making the gospel more familiar to people through its use in the sorts of rituals described in figure 13. Koinoniac music will emphasize affirmative and supportive themes in a ritual context.

C. Leitourgic Music

1. Field: What is to be communicated and what is being done

As was emphasized in the earlier discussion on the leitourgic mode, it comprises two moments which alternate in the rhythms of praise and prayer. Leitourgic music, too, has prayer music and praise music as its constituent elements. While spoken and unspoken prayer can never be displayed by sung prayer, sung prayer enables the presentation of the will's dispositions toward God to be more powerfully expressed. This may explain the popularity of musical versions of the Lord's Prayer for millions of people in the Western world. The other side of leitourgic music is the musical praise of God in which God is directly addressed and thanked. This is perhaps why James saw a distinction between praying and singing: "Is any one of you in trouble? He should pray. Is anyone happy? Let him sing songs of praise" (Jas. 5:13). While singing is most often associated with praise, it can still perform an invaluable function in the articulation of our needs before God (that is, as sung prayer).

Showing a similar division of praying and singing, Paul wrote in 1 Corinthians 14:15: "I will pray with my spirit, but I will also pray with my mind; I will sing with my spirit, but I will also sing with my mind." Apart from this distinction between singing and praying (which should not be construed as eliminating sung prayer), it is clear that Paul clearly recognized in this text the legitimacy of ecstatic prayer and singing alongside rational prayer and singing, understanding *rational* here to mean intelligible or comprehensible. Throughout this passage, however, he asserted that while both forms are valid, intelligible forms of prayer and song are of more value to the community when compared to the value to the individual of the unintelligible forms. This judgment is explicitly stated in 1 Corinthians 14:19; "But in the church I would rather speak five intelligible words to instruct others than ten thousand words in a tongue." Paul stressed here the edification which results from the exercise of spiritual gifts in an intelligible form, "with the mind." While "singing in the Spirit" was approved by Paul for individual edification, it is significant that the edification of the community falls within the boundaries of singing "with the mind."

2. Tenor: Degree of formality, intragroup relations, and appropriate dispositions of the will

Prayer music and praise music is formal in the sense that, as with kerygmatic music, there is no provision made (humanly speaking) for communication from God in the same mode as the congregation presents it (that is, by singing).

The group is nonspecialized from a musical point of view —it is not performing so as to be listened to as a musical performance. We remember Temperley's comment, "Hymns exist for the singers, not for an audience, still less for a critic."

In prayer we express a need for God. "Desolation" may be a rather strong way to express this need but it designates the bottom point in our need for God. Jubilation, on the other hand signifies the highest point of praise. Here we have received our request from God and our delight knows no inhibitions.

3. Mode: How the meanings are exchanged and what the song's function is

Continuing with the modifications to Nattiez's typology, it is possible to give it a "leitourgic" orientation. This is what Lomax has called a group-dominated musical event, as referred to earlier. Here both the producing or performing function and the interpreting function coalesce and become identical. There are two examples of this kind of structuring of the musical event. One is where a performer is practicing music on his or her own. This is a situation where the producing and interpreting functions coalesce within a single person. The other example of this type of musical event is when a congregation sings all together. The group is then producing and interpreting a given musical artifact by itself and for itself as a group. This is illustrated in figure 15.

Like the kerygmatic address-situation, leitourgic music is monodirectional—but in the other direction. In kerygmatic music God speaks to us through the singer. In leitourgic the singer speaks directly to God. The expectation is that God is listening. Leitourgic music is the place to speak directly to God. In the words of Theodore Jennings, there are many churches where the most important worship reform that can be imagined is "the careful and complete distinction between those words addressed to God and those addressed to the congregation."[38] It is rather amazing how many hymns and songs we customarily sing in church believing them to

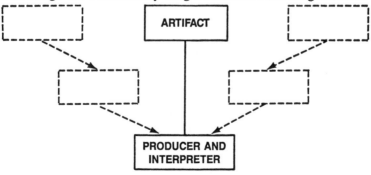

FIGURE 15:
A "LEITOURGIC" ORIENTATION TO THE FUNCTIONAL TRIPARTITION

be songs of praise, but in fact they are about God and not addressed to God. Biblically speaking, Christ has won us access directly to God, meaning we can "approach the throne of grace with confidence" (Heb. 4:16). This means face-to-face (metaphorically speaking) communion with God in our worship. Kerygmatic songs are about God, whereas leitourgic songs are directly addressed to God. All the pronouns must be first- and second-person singular and first-person plural in leitourgic music—I, you, me, we.

4. General Orientation of the Musical Style

Leitourgic music is the most resistant to change and, therefore, older styles remain firmly entrenched for generations. Witness the fright—maybe even panic—when our familiar worship routine is altered and we are asked to sing songs we don't know, songs in a unfamiliar melodic and harmonic idiom. Yet, strangely, in the kerygmatic mode, we would be dismayed if the choir did not learn new pieces and had only ten well-worn pieces in their repertoire! It takes a crisis of major proportions for any Christian community to alter the musical style of their worship songs.

In terms of general stylistic features, leitourgic music is the least complicated of the three modes. For musicians this can be a problem unless they understand it is music adapted to a different use. A secular rock musician who later became a Christian, told how the music of worship first appeared to him: "I wasn't used to simple music like this, but it blew me away! It was music that drew people into the Lord's presence! I loved it."[39] Whatever the style, leitourgic music must facilitate the declaration of our need and our love for God.

5. Level of Musical Replicability

This has already been covered under koinoniac music, where it was pointed out that the larger the group, the greater the spread of musical abilities, the lower the common musical denominator has to be. Joseph Gelineau, in a beautiful passage, described exactly what is needed for leitourgic music from a musical point of view:

> [It is] music not necessarily new and surprising in its language, not necessarily too difficult to perform, but so suited to what it is celebrating that it would be an inexhaustible source of prayer, meaning and feeling. . . . A music that was not full of itself but the bearer of silence and worship as Mary bore the incarnate Word.[40]

6. The Relationship of Leitourgic Music to Cultural Diversity

From what has been said before—the resistance to change in leitourgic music, the stylistic conservatism, and the need for it to be simple musically—it is clear that leitourgic music will tend to be the area where culturally diverse styles are least welcome. This is because it is in worship that the church is most basically and simply itself before God. Here it is most vulnerable and most dependent on God. Simplicity and familiarity with words and tune become essential as we approach the holy of holies, for "It is a dreadful thing to fall into the hands of the living God" (Heb. 10:31).

Conversely, segments of Christendom which are undergoing the most rapid liturgical innovation are those segments that are most open, initially, to culturally diverse musical styles. It has been interesting to observe in the charaismatic movement the openness—unusual in Western Christianity—for songs using Afro-American musical idioms and Israeli folk-musical idioms.

7. The Relationship of Leitourgic Music to the Address-Situation of Scripture

The leitourgic music of prayer will tend to use prayers or fragments of prayers as its scriptural base, while the leitourgic music of praise will use jubilant outbursts of worship. It is clear that the Book of Psalms would be an important sourcebook for both types of leitourgic music. Unfortunately, the Book of Psalms in its present form cannot be used directly for Christian hymnody. If it is Christian song, it has to conform to the criterion of Colossians 3:16—the word of Christ. It is not possible to draw near to Christ if we live on an exclusive diet of Old Testament psalms, as Isaac Watts realized only too well. That does not prevent an abundance of creative paraphrases, since the Psalms will always be the treasure house of Christian spirituality, as they were for our Lord.

8. The Relationship of Leitourgic Music to Rituals of Church and Community

When we want to emphasize our dependence on God or His nearness in our times of crisis, leitourgic music can function effectively in a ritual context. It can bring a vertical dimension to a ritual which can transform its predominantly horizontal orientation.

D. Additional Notes on the Model of Church Music

Before offering a few suggested applications of this model, I need to make a few additional comments on points not covered in the diagram.

1. Not every type of hymn or song can or should fit this model of church music. For example a large number of hymns and songs are calls to worship. These are an example of a *transitional* mode, moving the people from one activity to another. Calls to worship (as in the hymn, "Praise my Soul, the King of Heaven") are important and necessary but the frequent misuse of them is a cause for concern. I have often had the experience that due to a lack of awareness the whole service was one long call to worship. After a brief call to worship, we must worship God, as called for in leitourgic music. In worship, as stated earlier, we stop singing *about* God and start singing *to* God.

There are other songs which do not fit the three modes of church music. Sometimes a part of the song will fit, but another part won't. This is usually because the hymn or songwriter changed viewpoint halfway through the hymn. A good example of this is Wesley's famous hymn, "Hark! The Herald Angels Sing." If you examine the full ten-verse version, you will notice that it is a peculiar mixture—the first six verses are kerygmatic and the last four are leitourgic. The poet has changed his viewpoint halfway through the poem, which makes it hard to fit into the typology I have proposed. This is not necessarily a defect in either Wesley's hymn or my typology, but just an observation. Still, it is preferable for a song to have a consistent treatment all the way through.[41]

2. It is not necessary to think of the three modes of church music operating only on a Sunday. Preferably, a service should have all three types in one service, but the opportunities to use the three types outside Sunday services are many. There are many places far from the church where kerygmatic music can be used. Koinoniac music can be used in many informal, nonworship church meetings. The use of leitourgic music can also be broadened to include its use in home fellowships and one's private devotions.

3. Those who play instruments may feel that I have neglected them in this model of church music. Not so—I believe instrumentalists have a vital role to play in church music. However, in general, it is a supportive and subsidiary role. The reason has been well stated by Joseph Gelineau: "Singing has a privileged position in the Christian liturgy because of its connection with the revealed word. Only singing can combine explicit confession of faith in Christ with musical expression."[42] Obviously instrumental music can and should be used for its own sake in the church—this is part of the general cultural mandate with regard to the music discussed in the section on "Music and Creation." Yet its greatest contribution is to enhance the central process of letting the word of Christ dwell richly in our hearts through song. What a marvelous asset instruments can be in this high and holy task! They do not lose dignity in this role, but rather gain it.

4. What evidence is there for the validity of this model? Support for it comes from two sources: hymnology and contemporary Christian music.

In Louis Benson's classic textbook on hymnology published in 1927 entitled *The Hymnody of the Christian Church,* you will find that he analyzed the different types of hymn. His types, doctrinal, didactic, doctrinal lyric, sermonic, and hymns of personal experience, can be classified as kerygmatic. The types he called church militant and church triumphant are koinoniac. He made a place for hymns of prayer and praise, which accounts for the leitourgic mode.

Moving on to 1980, we find a similar division in Eskew and McElrath's textbook on hymnody, *Sing with Understanding* (Broadman). They devote separate chapters to the following: "The Hymn in Proclamation," "The Hymn in Worship," "The Hymn in Education," "The Hymn in Ministry." I prefer rather to place the ministry of education under proclamation since both presuppose a similar type of address-situation. This reduces their four categories of hymn usage to three and fits exactly with the model of church music: proclamation=kerygmatic; worship=leitourgic; ministry=koinoniac.

Even though these two treatises on hymnology are separated by more than fifty years, they both yield an approach to the songs of the church which dovetail with the model of church music proposed.

Our second source of support for the model comes from contemporary Christian music. Paul Baker in his excellent history of this style of music talked about the vital role of praise music (which he called "vertical") in the lives of the many rock musicians who became Christians as a result of the Jesus movement. While they were more used to "horizontal" message music, they learned to love the vertical praise music.[43] Greg Volz talked recently in an interview about two types of Christian music—praise music and relational music.[44] Steve Camp, also in a recent interview, distinguished between music which comforts (he used Amy Grant as an example) and music which confronts (Keith Green's *No Compromise* album).[45]

My point in listing these three statements about uses of music is that if one takes them altogether, they match the model of church music. Praise music is obviously leitourgic, music which comforts is koinoniac, and confrontative and relational music is kerygmatic.

I believe it is significant that from such widely differing viewpoints the threefold model of church music still finds confirmation. Yet the test of any theory is not whether people agree with it. The test is whether can it make a difference in practice, in the "real" world? I believe it can and will attempt to demonstrate this now.

E. Applications of the Model To Church Music

I believe this model can help in the following ways:

1. Different traditions in the church tend to develop their church music according to how they conceptualize the task of the church. Evangelistically minded churches restrict themselves largely to kerygmatic music, while churches stressing "body-life" versions of Christianity are largely confined to koinoniac music. In churches where worship is the predominant interest, the focus is almost exclusively on leitourgic music. The results of such unbalanced and unbiblical approaches is a musical and, above all, a Christian impoverishment. This impoverishment results directly from truncated and myopic theologies of the church and its mission. It can be easily overcome if we accept that all three types of church music—kerygmatic, koinoniac, and leitourgic—have a legitimate place in the church. They are all valid and need to be used regularly, creatively, systematically, and carefully.

2. This model can provide a helpful stimulus to composers and songwriters. They need to be aware of the context in which church music operates. Far from being a confining straitjacket, I believe this model of church music can open up exciting new possibilities for creative writers.

3. Finally, this model can guide church musicians in choosing materials. It can function as a tool to help the musical decision maker answer the question: what goal does music need to facilitate in this situation? Is it proclamation, affirmation, or worship? Just to distinguish between songs appropriate to these three functions is a major step forward.

But it can offer greater refinements. It will help us to analyze the texts of songs, to analyze the music and see if both together are appropriate to the situation required. This model enables one to coordinate a specific musical choice with a specific situation. For example, a kerygmatic song will not fit in a koinoniac situation, since the two address-situations are radically different. In the same way, use of this model will help us not to confuse the koinoniac and the leitourgic mode.

I recently participated in a meeting where the musical leadership was trying to be vertical (praise) and horizontal (fellowship) at the same time! Needless to say it did not work, and there was much confusion as to the whole event. As we learn how to use the model on a more consistent basis, we can have confidence that our music is definitely contributing to the mission of the church and is part of God's redemptive plan for our world. Although musical aspects of the church's life may be misunderstood and maligned, often by the ignorant, it does have an absolutely vital part to play in the life of the church. No matter what the difficulties, we have to move forward. The model of church music gives us a workable way of doing just that.

In conclusion, consider this quotation from a noted theologian where he emphasized the great importance of church music. It is a high calling and it deserves our best efforts.

> What we can and must say quite confidently is that the community which does not sing is not the community. And where it cannot sing in living speech, or only archaically in repetition of the modes and texts of the past; where it does not really sing but signs and mumbles spasmodically, shamefacedly and with an ill grace, it can be at best only a troubled community which is not sure of its cause and of whose ministry and witness there can be no great expectation. . . . The praise of God which finds its concrete culmination in the singing of the community is one of the indispensible basic forms of the ministry of the community.[46]

Notes

1. Martin Hengel, "Hymns and Christology," *Between Jesus and Paul* (London: SCM Press, 1983) p. 79.

2. Hengel, p. 80.

3. Peter O'Brien, *Word Biblical Commentary: Colossians, Philemon,* Vol 44 (Waco: World Books, 1982) p. 206.

4. Martin Hengel, "Hymns and Christology," p. 80.

5. *Ibid.*

6. O'Brien, pp. 207-208.

7. Hengel, p. 79.

8. O'Brien, pp. 207, 208.

9. K. H. Bartels, "Song, Hymn, Psalm," *New International Dictionary of New Testament Theology*, Vol III, ed. C. Brown (Grand Rapids: Zondervan Publishing Company, 1978) 668; Martin Hengel, Hymns and Christology, pp. 80, 90-93.

10. G. Delling, *Worship in the New Testament* (London: Darton, Longman and Todd, 1962) 86.

11. E. Lohse, *Colossians and Philemon: Hermeneia*, ed. H. Koester (Philadelphia: Fortress Press, 1971) 151.

12. Lohse, p. 80.

13. Hengel, p. 80.

14. O'Brien, p. 210.

15. Hengel, p. 80.

16. O'Brien, p. 210.

17. H. Schlier, *Theological Dictionary of the New Testament*, Vol I, ed. G. Kittel (Grand Rapids: Wm. B. Eerdmans, 1964) p. 165.

18. George H. Lewis, "Cultural Socialization and the Development of Taste Cultures and Culture Classes in American Popular Music," *Popular Music and Society*, Vol 4, No. 4, 1976, 226-241.

19. M. A. K. Halliday, *Language as Social Semiotic* (London: Edward Arnold, 1978) p. 35.

20. Nicholas Temperley, *The Music of the English Parish Church*, Vol I (Cambridge: Cambridge University Press, 1979) 347.

21. P. Davies, "Boldness," *Interpreter's Dictionary of the Bible*, Vol I, ed. G. Buttrick (Nashville: Abingdon Press, 1962) 453.

22. The terminology "group-dominating" and "group-dominated" comes from Alan Lomax's pioneering study of folk-song styles, *Folk Song Style and Culture* (Washington: American Association for the Advancement of Science, 1968) 16. See also Frank L. Harrison, "Universals in Music: Towards a Methodology of Comparative Research," *World of Music*, Vol 19, No 1-2, 1977, 30-36.

23. Otto Laske, *Music, Memory and Thought* (Ann Arbor: University Microfilms, 1977) 90.

24. Laske, p. 298.

25. Hans Küng, *The Church* (London: Search Press, 1968) vii, viii.

26. Ethelbert Stauffer, *Theological Dictionary of the New Testament*, Vol II, ed. G. Kittel (Grand Rapids: Wm. B. Eerdmans, 1964) pp. 440, 441.

27. Stauffer, p. 442.

28. Hengel, "Between Jesus and Paul," *Between Jesus and Paul* (London: SCM Press, 1983) 1-27, see p. 14.

29. *Ibid.*

30. *Ibid.*

31. See, for example, Norma McLeod, "Ethnomusicological Research and Anthropology," *Annual Review of Anthropology*, Vol III, 1974, pp. 99-115.

32. Edmund Leach, *Culture and Communication* (Cambridge University Press, 1976) p. 77.

33. Anthony Wallace, *Religion: An Anthropological View* (New York: Random House, 1966) p. 106.*

34. Erik Routley, *Church Music and the Christian Faith*, revd. ed. (Carol Stream: Agape, 1978) pp. 90-91.

35. See Franky Schaeffer, *Addicted to Mediocrity* (Westchester: Cornerstone Books, 1981) for an example of such an approach.

36. William Harris, "Sounding Brass" and Hellenistic Technology," *Biblical Archaeology Review*, Vol VIII, No. 1, Jan/Feb. 1982, 38-42, see p. 42.

37. Carlton Young, quoted in Donald Hustad, *Jubilate!* (Carol Stream: Hope Publishing Company, 1981) p. 16.

38. Theodore Jennings, *Life as Worship* (Wm. B. Eerdmans, 1982) p. 44.

39. Quoted in Paul Baker, *Contemporary Christian Music* (Westchester: Crossway Books, 1985) p. 40.

40. Joseph Gelineau, *The Liturgy Today and Tomorrow* (London: Darton, Longman and Todd, 1978) p. 92.

41. Modern students of songwriting stress this, for example, Sheila Davis, *The Craft of Lyric Writing* (Cincinnati: Writer's Digest Books, 1985) pp. 82-98.

42. Joseph Gelineau, "Music and Singing in the Liturgy," *The Study of Liturgy*, ed. C. Jones, G. Wainwright and E. Yarnold (London: S.P.C.K. 1978) p. 443.

43. Paul Baker, *Contemporary Christian Music*, pp. 40-41.

44. Devlin Donaldson, Interview with Greg Volz, *Contemporary Christian Magazine*, September 1986, p. 24.

45. Thom Granger, Interview with Steven Camp, *Contemporary Christian Music Magazine*, November 1986, p. 21.

46. Karl Barth, *Church Dogmatics*, Vol IV, Part 3, Second Half (Edinburgh: T and T. Clark 1962) p. 867.

* See Lauri Honko, "Theories Concerning the Ritual Process," *Science of Religion: Studies in Methodology* (The Hague: Mouton Publishers, 1979) pp. 369-390 for a good discussion of calendrical and noncalendrical rituals.